The Government as Robin Hood

Exploring the Myth

The Government as Robin Hood

Exploring the Myth

G. C. RUGGERI

D. VAN WART

R. HOWARD

THE SCHOOL OF POLICY STUDIES
QUEEN'S UNIVERSITY

CALEDON INSTITUTE OF SOCIAL POLICY

Canadian Cataloguing in Publication Data

Ruggeri, G. C., 1943–
    The government as Robin Hood : exploring the myth

Co-published by the Caledon Institute of Social Policy.
Includes bibliographical references.
ISBN 0-88911-711-X

1. Income distribution – Canada. 2. Fiscal policy – Canada.
I. Van Wart, Donald C. (Donald Charles), 1953–   .
II. Howard, R. (Robert), 1954–   . III. Queen's University
(Kingston, Ont.). School of Policy Studies. IV. Caledon
Institute of Social Policy. V. Title.

HC120.I5R84 1996   339.5'2'0971   C96-930123-5

Contents

List of Tables and Figures

FIGURES

Acknowledgements

A project like this usually leaves a large debt of gratitude. We thank senior management at Alberta Treasury for providing an atmosphere conducive to research on public policy. We thank Monique Jerome-Forget for encouragement to undertake this project and France St-Hilaire, Bill Scarth, Mark Lisac and a number of anonymous referees for helpful suggestions. Ken Battle and Keith Banting have done an excellent job in bringing this study to publication. We also thank Maria Morrison and Lori Gale of Alberta Treasury for excellent staff support.

It should be emphasized that the study reflects the personal views of the authors and should not be construed as representing the position of Alberta Treasury. Finally, the authors alone are responsible for any errors or omissions.

G.C. Ruggeri
D. Van Wart
R. Howard

Introduction

Every government action affects the economic position of individuals and families, directly or indirectly, by design or by default. Governments can acknowledge and incorporate these effects in the design of programs. If they choose to ignore them, they risk serious political problems. The redistributional implications of government policy matter to people.

Individual government programs do not operate in a vacuum. Each program is part of the overall thrust of government activity and interacts with the other components of the fiscal system. Policymakers ideally need information on both the redistributional impact of each program and its relationship to the overall degree of fiscal redistribution.

Fiscal redistribution raises significant equity issues. It may also affect economic efficiency because changes in marginal tax and benefit rates and in the relative economic position of different groups may influence their economic behaviour. It is important to know not only how much redistribution is delivered by a given program, but also the associated gain or loss in economic efficiency.

This volume was prepared as a contribution to our understanding of the redistributional impact of government activity. It presents estimates of the extent to which the fiscal system of the three orders of government in Canada affected the economic position of different income and demographic groups in 1986.

The first chapter includes background material. It provides a summary comparison of fiscal redistribution studies in a number of countries including Canada, the US, the UK and Sweden. Since the results of those empirical studies are affected by differences in methodology, we explain the major assumptions used in our calculations in Chapter 1 and provide a detailed summary in the Appendix. Additional details on our methodology and results are found in a companion volume which is available from the authors as an Alberta Treasury Research Paper (Ruggeri, Van Wart and Howard 1994).

Our estimates of fiscal incidence are presented and discussed in the subsequent two chapters. Chapter 2 deals with the redistributional impact of the entire budget. The vertical equity dimensions of fiscal redistribution are shown first for all governments combined and then separately by order of government. We also compare the net fiscal gains and losses of five household types divided into four major income classes. In Chapter 3 we present details on the redistributional impact of taxes, government purchases and transfer payments. The results presented in Chapters 2 and 3 challenge a number of traditional views on fiscal redistribution.

Chapter 4 establishes a link between redistribution and equity. The purpose of redistribution is to reduce the degree of income inequality. Therefore, one expects that the degree of redistribution increases with the degree of inequality that would exist under a redistributionally neutral fiscal regime. We tested this hypothesis by relating the change in income inequality caused by fiscal redistribution to the income inequality in the absence of redistribution for each of the five household types. We also tested the hypothesis that redistribution reduced the degree of inequality among household types.

Our results provide estimates of the redistributional impact of one part of government activity only, namely government spending and taxation. The scope of government extends well beyond budgetary actions. Non-budgetary activity, such as regulation and enforcement of property rights, may produce redistribution in a direction opposite to that of the fiscal system. If the non-fiscal component tends to increase the degree of income inequality, then fiscal redistribution in favour of the poor may be considered partly a form of indemnity. It is important to evaluate the redistributional implications of both the fiscal and non-fiscal activities of government. For practical purposes, it may be more fruitful if this evaluation is carried out separately and then the results compared. We hope that the presentation of our results on the fiscal side stimulates research on the non-fiscal side.

The insights gained from the results provide some guidance for a general evaluation of alternative approaches to redistribution. In Chapter 5 we suggest a change in direction for redistributional policy that would improve efficiency in the provision of a given degree of redistribution.

Our findings indicate that, without the redistributional impact of government spending and taxation, the income distribution in 1986 would have been quite unequal. The fiscal system reduced considerably the degree of inequality of earnings.

Total redistribution, as measured by the sum of the gains received by those who benefited from the fiscal system, was $58.4 billion, including the benefits of the $20.5 billion deficit incurred in 1986. This is equivalent to 25 cents per dollar of government expenditure. The poor (households with income below 50 percent of the median) received 45 percent of this amount. The low-income class (those with incomes between 50 percent and 75 percent of the median) received 34 percent. Each dollar of government spending provided 11 cents of redistribution in favour of the poor and another 8.5 cents in favour of the low-income class.

The middle class (those with income between 75 percent and 150 percent of the median) also received substantial benefits from the fiscal system. Its gross gain amounted to $10.5 billion, equal to 40 percent of the gain by the poor (18 percent of total gains). This gain was split between all lower middle-class family types ($7.3 billion) and upper middle-class seniors ($3.1 billion). Part of this gain was offset by losses by upper middle-income singles and one and two income families with two parents; the net gain to the middle class was $4.1 billion, or 7 percent of the total. These numbers show that there was a considerable amount of redistribution within the middle class. The middle class received 33.5 percent of transfer payments, almost equal to its share of households (36.9 percent).

The biggest losses in total dollars from fiscal redistribution were incurred by high-income singles and couples, with a combined loss of $11.5 billion, one-third of the total gains. An additional loss of $12 billion, or 20 percent of the total gain, was incurred by the rich.

Our results also show that there was as much indirect, and perhaps unintended, redistribution through the provision of public and social goods as from the more direct vehicle of transfer payments to persons.

Approximately one-quarter of each dollar of transfers to persons was received by the poor. One-third of total transfers was received by the middle class. For the middle class, transfer payments represented 25 cents out of each dollar paid in taxes. The transfer payments system in 1986 operated more as an insurance scheme than as Robin Hood.

Finally, our findings show that taxation was a more powerful instrument of redistribution than either government purchases or transfer payments. Its redistributive power, however, was confined to the personal income tax. These results call into question, on redistributive grounds, proposals for reducing the redistributional role of taxation, for example, by lowering the progressivity of the personal income tax.

We do not address the issue of whether the fiscal system generates too much or too little redistribution. We question, however, the efficiency of an approach to redistribution which accepts uncritically market processes and then tries simply to correct socially undesirable distributional outcomes. In a democratic society, with an aversion to inequality, it may be more efficient to prevent wide disparities in private earnings than to correct them with *ex post* adjustments. We propose a shift from programs of passive corrective redistribution to active preventive redistribution. This shift involves a move away from unconditional payments that generate disincentives to productive activity and towards a policy that improves equality of opportunity, breaks down discriminatory barriers and actively promotes high employment.

Since our results are based on 1986 data, we have added a postscript that discusses the probable impact on fiscal redistribution of the changes in Canadian tax and expenditure policies from 1986 to 1995. We conclude that the recent moves to balance budgets and reform transfers to persons programs have not significantly altered our results.

CHAPTER ONE

Why and How We Measure
Fiscal Redistribution

WHY FISCAL REDISTRIBUTION STUDIES

The role of government in redistributing income has become a central focus of current political debate. This is partly a response to stagnant family incomes during the past decade and growing earnings inequality.[1] It also reflects concerns over large government deficits[2] and the appropriate mix of tax and expenditure policies required to bring budgets into balance. Fairness is a well-worn theme in discussions concerning the personal income tax and consumption taxes,[3] but has not been applied as frequently in the analysis of public spending.

In the absence of detailed studies on the incidence of taxation and government spending, public policy is designed in a vacuum with respect to its redistributional impact. When we began this project, the available Canadian fiscal incidence studies were based on data that are more than 20 years old. In the past 20 years, the federal and provincial tax systems have changed considerably. Government spending on goods and services as a proportion of total expenditures has declined and the share of direct transfers has increased. Most of the available fiscal incidence studies provide estimates only by income classes, preventing an evaluation of fiscal redistribution by type of household. In addition, significant advances have been made with respect to both methodology and the quality of data. We found the need for an updated study of fiscal redistribution in Canada compelling. We hope that the results will be helpful in the ongoing debate on the size and function of government.

Our study sheds some light on the following questions: How much income is redistributed by the fiscal policies of Canadian government? How are the benefits and losses distributed among income groups and family types? Which order of

TABLE 1-1: International Comparison of Fiscal Redistribution Studies

Country	Author and Year	Major Conclusions
Canada	Gillespie, W. Irwin (1966)	Using data for 1961, taxation was overall mildly progressive, although slightly regressive at the top and bottom. Transfers and government purchases were both progressive. Hence, the overall fiscal system was progressive, although there was negative redistribution over the upper income classes.
Ontario, Canada	Johnson, James A. (1968)	For 1961 data. Similar conclusions to Gillespie; the provincial tax regime was somewhat regressive and transfers were quite progressive.
Canada	Dodge, David A. (1975)	For 1970. Broadly similar to Gillespie; found that federal budgetary policies of the early 1970s favoured high income families.
Canada	Gillespie, W. Irwin (1980a)	Compared results for 1969 with 1961. Concluded that government policy had become somewhat more beneficial to the poor and considerably more beneficial to the rich in the 1960s.
Canada	Gillespie, W. Irwin (1980b)	Compared 1969 results adjusted to 1977 with earlier results back to 1951. Same conclusions.
Quebec, Canada	Payette, M. and Vaillancourt, F. (1986)	The 1981 Quebec tax system was regressive, while transfers and government purchases were progressive. Overall fiscal redistribution was slightly progressive.
Canada	Horry, I. and Walker, M. (1994)	For six periods from 1969 to 1980. Concluded that government taxation is highly progressive, transfers were progressive and that government purchases were regressive. Taxation has become more progressive while spending progressivity has changed little since 1969. The fiscal regime was overall progressive.
United States	Musgrave, R.A., Case, K.E. and Leonard, H. (1974)	Using 1968 data, the tax system was found to be mildly progressive overall, with state and local taxes being regressive. Both transfers and purchases benefits were highly progressive at lower incomes. The overall fiscal system was progressive.
United States	Reynolds, M. and Smolensky, E. (1977)	Uses data for 1950, 1961 and 1970. Similar to above. Federal taxes were found to be mildly progressive, although less so in 1970; state and local taxes were regressive, becoming more so in 1970. Overall taxes were progressive in each year. Expenditures were quite progressive; federal expenditures progressivity increased, while state and local declined. Overall, fiscal regime was progressive, but less so in 1970.

... continued

TABLE 1-1 *(continued)*

Country	Author and Year	Major Conclusions
United States	Ruggles, P. and O'Higgins, M. (1981)	Using 1970 data, federal taxes were found to be largely proportional while state and local taxes were slightly regressive. Overall, taxes were regressive. Expenditure benefits, both transfers and purchases, were highly progressive. Total fiscal benefits were quite progressive.
United Kingdom	O'Higgins, M. and Ruggles, P. (1981)	Using 1971 data, they use more complete tax and benefit allocations than CSO studies. Taxes are found to be largely proportional and somewhat progressive at the top. Transfers and expenditure benefits are much less progressive than in CSO analysis. Net fiscal benefits are overall progressive.

government has the largest redistributional impact? Which of the three major components of the budget — taxation, transfers to persons and government purchases for social goods — is the most powerful instrument of redistribution? How much is the inequality of private income reduced by the fiscal system?

The remainder of Chapter 1 has two sections. The first provides a survey of the major conclusions of fiscal redistribution studies for Canada and other countries. These can be used as benchmarks for comparison with our results. The second explains how a fiscal incidence study is done, highlighting five important methodological issues that also serve to delineate the special features of this study.

SURVEY OF FISCAL REDISTRIBUTION STUDIES

Studies of the redistributional impact of the fiscal system are available for several countries. In this section we discuss the results of relatively recent fiscal redistribution studies for Canada and offer a brief survey of results for other countries. A summary of these studies for Canada, the United States and the United Kingdom is found in Table 1-1.

Canada

Studies for the entire Canadian fiscal system include Gillespie (1966, 1980), Dodge (1975), and Horry and Walker (1994); there is also a study by Johnson (1968) for Ontario and Payette and Vaillancourt (1986) for Quebec. A survey of Canadian tax and fiscal incidence studies is found in Dahlby (1985).

In his first study, prepared for the Royal Commission on Taxation (the Carter Commission), Gillespie (1966, p. 189) concluded that "the public sector affects positive income redistribution — by income class — over the lower income ranges, and negative income redistribution over the upper income classes." Gillespie (1980a) later repeated the exercise with 1969 data and analyzed the changes that occurred since 1961. He found that "During 1969 there was redistribution from the higher income classes to the lower income classes" (p. 170). His result also showed that "during the 1960s the total fiscal system became somewhat more beneficial to the poor and considerably more beneficial to the rich, mostly at the expense of upper-middle income units" (p. 171).

In a separate study, Gillespie (1978) analyzed the redistributional effects of federal budgetary changes introduced during the 1970s and reached a different conclusion. He found that "federal budgetary policies during the 1970s have more often than not generated larger benefits for the highest-income families than for the poor" (p. 24). These results are also presented in a comparison of fiscal incidence from 1951 to 1977 in Gillespie (1980b).[5]

Dodge followed a methodology similar to Gillespie's, but included the federal reform of the income tax in 1971, of unemployment insurance in 1972 and of family allowances in 1973, as well as the higher old age pension and guaranteed income supplement in 1973. He concurred with Gillespie that the 1970 incidence of the combined tax and spending programs of all levels of government was broadly redistributive in favour of low income families, but found that the effect of the federal reforms of the early 1970s "increased the amount of redistribution from the rich to the poor" (p. 1).

After the completion of the study presented in this volume, Horry and Walker (1994) published the first full fiscal incidence study for Canada in 20 years, for 1990. They also provide consistent fiscal incidence calculations for 1970, 1975, 1980, 1985 and 1988. Estimates are provided for the combined and three orders of government, for the provinces and territories, and for families by ten income classes, by deciles and by age.[4] In addition, Horry and Walker present the first lifetime fiscal incidence estimates for Canada. They conclude that the tax system and government transfers to persons are highly progressive, and that government spending on social goods, especially health and education, are regressive.

Unlike the other Canadian studies cited, Horry and Walker use an incomplete and inconsistent income base by including government transfers to persons, but not government spending on goods and services.[5] Unlike all other fiscal studies cited, they show only the absolute distribution of the tax and expenditure dollars, rather than the ratio of these to income, which provides a burden measure of fiscal incidence.[6] Absolute fiscal incidence does not express fiscal burdens and benefits relative to income and, hence, provides no information on redistribution. It also does not provide a revenue-neutral comparison between taxes and expenditures. For these reasons, the results are not directly comparable to other studies and may lead to misinterpretation about the progressivity of a budget component.[7]

Johnson estimated the incidence of spending and taxation by the three orders of government in Ontario in 1961. His results concurred with Gillespie's and Dodge's findings for Canada; government fiscal activity generally redistributed income from higher to lower income classes. The same conclusion was reached by Payette and Vaillancourt regarding the effects of the Quebec fiscal system in 1981.

All of the above studies, except Horry and Walker (1994), found that the redistribution of income generated by the fiscal system results largely from the progressive (pro-poor) distribution of government transfers to persons. Taxation was found to be roughly proportional or mildly regressive and government spending on social goods was found to be mildly progressive.

US Studies

Three major studies of fiscal redistribution in the United States include Musgrave, Case and Leonard (1974); Reynolds and Smolensky (1977); and Ruggles and O'Higgins (1981).

Musgrave, Case and Leonard's estimates are for 1968. Combined fiscal incidence was significantly progressive with the break-even point occurring at the median income, dividing the population about evenly between gainers and losers. The federal fisc was much more progressive than the state and local fisc. The combined state and local tax system was found to be regressive and the federal tax system progressive. Transfers were the most progressive element of fiscal policy.

Reynolds and Smolensky published detailed estimates of fiscal incidence for 1950, 1961 and 1970. They agreed with Musgrave *et al.* that the fisc redistributed income in favour of the poor; they found, however, that the US fiscal regime was less progressive in 1970 than in the earlier years. During the 1950-70 period, federal expenditure progressivity increased, due to the higher share of cash transfers, but federal tax progressivity fell. The combined state and local fiscal systems became less progressive on both the tax and spending side.

A later study by Ruggles and O'Higgins, also for 1970, concluded that federal taxes overall were essentially proportional and that combined federal, state and local taxes were slightly regressive. This regressivity was offset by a high degree of progressivity of expenditures, both transfers and purchases. The net result was a progressive fiscal incidence.

Other Countries

In the United Kingdom, the Central Statistical Office (CSO) has published partial fiscal incidence estimates for every year since 1957. These estimates allocate about two-thirds of government revenue and one-half of government expenditures, shying away from allocating the more controversial components. They find that overall taxes, transfers and government purchases are all consistently progressive, with most of the redistribution being generated by transfers. Over time, the tax system and overall fiscal regime have become somewhat less progressive, especially since 1977.

O'Higgins and Ruggles, in a companion study to that for the US, allocated all revenues and expenditures of the UK government for 1971. Their conclusions were similar to those of their US study. Taxes overall were found to be essentially proportional, although somewhat regressive at the top. Transfers and, especially, purchases were found to be much less progressive than the CSO estimates. The overall fisc was still moderately progressive.

A study by Franzén, Lövgren and Rosenberg (1975) estimated the net fiscal incidence of government in Sweden separately for married-couple households and single-parent households for 1970. Their estimates indicate that, unlike the previously cited studies for Canada, the US and UK, the tax system was highly progressive over all income ranges. Combined with quite progressive transfers and government purchases, the Swedish fisc appears to generate substantially more redistribution than in Canada, the US, or UK.

Evidence on fiscal redistribution in a number of other countries comes from only partial studies, with no complete study of net fiscal incidence.

A fiscal incidence study for Australia by Harding (1984) included direct and indirect taxes, and expenditures for social security programs, education, health and housing for 1975-76. The study concluded that combined taxes are broadly proportional to income, cash transfers are highly progressive, the other government expenditures are less progressive and overall fiscal incidence is progressive.

For Germany, studies by Krupp (1983) for 1975 and by the Deutches Institut für Wirtschaftsforschung (1983) for 1981 estimated the fiscal incidence of direct taxes, transfers and selected public services. Both studies show quite progressive transfers, highly progressive direct taxes, and only moderately progressive purchases.

Foulon and Hatchuel (1979) analyzed the redistribution of income between households on the basis of the occupation of the household head in France for 1965 and 1970. They allocate about three-quarters of taxes, 90 percent of transfers and public education spending. Although the approach is less comparable to the other studies, transfers appear mildly progressive, public education somewhat regressive and taxes largely proportional.

The Irish Central Statistical Office (CSO) produced a study comparable to the British CSO, with partial revenues and expenditures, for 1973. The results are discussed by Nolan (1981) and O'Connell (1982). It found that taxes were largely proportional, with some regressivity at the top and bottom of the income distribution, transfers were quite progressive, and purchases were highly progressive. In the case of purchases, education was somewhat regressive, while health care was markedly progressive.

The results of a study by Denmark Statistics on fiscal redistribution among employed households, including taxes, transfers and the benefits of health and daycare services, for 1963 and 1971 are reported by Bjerke and Brodersen (1978). Taxes overall were largely proportional, but progressive at higher incomes, transfers were markedly progressive and health and daycare services were somewhat progressive. They conclude that there is substantial net fiscal redistribution.

Finally, Suominen (1979) reports on a study by Official Statistics of Finland of fiscal incidence for 1971 that includes all taxes and transfers plus expenditures for social services (including education, health, recreation and welfare). The overall tax system, like Sweden, appears highly progressive, especially for higher income classes, transfers are quite progressive and the social services are moderately progressive. This indicates substantial net fiscal redistribution from higher to lower income groups.

MAJOR METHODOLOGICAL ISSUES

Database

A notable feature of this study is the use of a highly detailed micro database developed by Statistics Canada — the Social Policy Simulation Database/Model (SPSD/M).[8] The SPSD/M micro database consists of a simulated sample of over 100,000 individuals in their family contexts. It incorporates extensive details on demographic composition, income sources, employment status, education and expenditures.

The SPSD/M database is constructed from four statistical and administrative microdata files: the Survey of Consumer Finances, personal income tax returns, unemployment insurance claims histories, and the Family Expenditure Survey. These files are augmented with aggregate data, used to provide benchmarks or control totals, from the 1981 and 1986 census, Canada Assistance Plan administrative reports, Statistics Canada's *Vital Statistics*, and Department of Health and Welfare summary reports. The core dataset is the Survey of Consumer Finances. Various statistical techniques were used to augment this micro data with the other data sources.

The households in the SPSD/M database are synthetic in the sense that the information on each household comes from at least four different households. The data contains a considerable amount of manufactured information, especially for the very low and very high income groups. For example, certain income components, such as social assistance, are calculated through statistical algorithms, and statistical blurring is used at high and low incomes. In addition, the four datasets are statistically matched each time the model is run, so that the synthetic households are slightly different in every run.

In theory, given the availability of a sufficiently detailed, actual microdata set, it would be preferable to calculate fiscal incidence measures for each household and, then, aggregate into selected income-demographic groups. In practice, this may not be the best approach. We chose to first aggregate the data into 330 families, defined by income and demographic characteristics, and then adjust these composite families, as suggested in the SPSD/M manual.

There are four reasons for adopting this approach over the alternative of making detailed adjustments to each household within the SPSD/M model. First, while individual household calculations allow the measurement of fiscal redistribution within groups, the estimates would be quite unreliable given the small sample size of certain groups. Second, the quality of the data is not uniform at all income levels or for all family types and, as mentioned above, the micro data is not strictly provided at the household level.

Third, the SPSD/M does not provide a ready-made database for fiscal incidence analysis. As explained in the tax incidence studies by Vermaeten, Gillespie and Vermaeten (1994) and Ruggeri, Van Wart and Howard (1994a), substantial alterations and additions are required, particularly with respect to accrued and imputed income, before it can be used for tax incidence analysis. The data for these alterations are available only for large aggregates. Similarly, the SPSD/M contains no information on government purchases. The benefits of government purchases are allocated by income class and family type using assumptions adopted from the public finance literature. Allocating those benefits to individual households would not increase the accuracy of the results. If each household is assigned the average value of government benefits in the group, the detailed calculation of fiscal incidence yields the same result as the use of the representative member.

For these reasons, we divided the total households in the database into 330 groups, composed of 22 income classes and 15 family types. This procedure is equivalent to selecting the average household in each group. It provides a policy-relevant population breakdown and allows a reasonable cell count for each group. We then made a number of adjustments to the database. Each income component was independently adjusted to conform to Statistics Canada's national income and expenditure account totals for 1986. This allowed the value of SPSD/M total income to be expanded to include non-money private income imputations, taxes that are assumed to be shifted backwards to factors of production and government expenditures on public and social goods. In addition, the distribution of various imputed and government goods components of income were based on distributions from various other data sources, including Statistics Canada's Financial Management System accounts.

Income Concept

Two consistent income concepts can be used for the measurement of tax or fiscal incidence: pre-fisc income and actual post-fisc income. Pre-fisc income is a hypothetical measure of private factor income in the absence of government. It can also be interpreted as the special case of post-fisc income associated with a distributionally neutral budget. We refer to this income concept as neutral-fisc income. Post-fisc income is a comprehensive measure of a family's command over resources. It measures income from all sources, including transfer payments and the benefits of government purchases, minus taxes assigned to that family.

The choice between the two income bases has little effect on the pattern of overall fiscal incidence, but alters considerably the pattern of incidence of each budget component. Specifically, under the neutral-fisc concept, taxes appear to be either less progressive (pro-poor) or more regressive (pro-rich), while expenditures appear to be more progressive or less regressive.

Our study used actual post-fisc income. In our view it offers a more intuitive interpretation of fiscal and tax incidence results and provides a more appropriate counterfactual. The superiority of post-fisc income over neutral-fisc income in measuring the redistributional impact of each budget component has been emphasized by Lambert (1985) and Lambert and Pfähler (1986). Actual post-fisc income provides an estimate of the standard of living, or potential consumption, of households in the period under consideration (not taking into account differences in the consumption of leisure). The ratio of taxes paid to post-fisc income indicates the degree by which the current standard of living (including the benefits received when the tax revenue is spent) is reduced by the payment of taxes. The same interpretation applies to the ratio of the benefits of government spending to post-fisc income.[9]

Only the use of either neutral-fisc or post-fisc income allows the derivation of the measure of fiscal redistribution as the sum of the impacts of taxes, purchases and transfers. Such a consistent decomposition cannot be obtained when the income concept includes only pre-fisc income plus transfer payments (partial post-fisc income), an income measure often used in tax incidence studies.[10] A major shortcoming of partial post-fisc income is that it yields different patterns of tax incidence for identical tax structures, depending on the relative share of transfer payments in total government expenditures. For example, if transfers to universities were replaced by direct transfers of equal value to university students, the pattern of tax incidence based on partial post-fisc income would change, even if the tax structure was unaffected.

It should be noted that post-fisc income is more difficult to measure than either pre- or partial post-fisc income because of the difficulty in allocating the benefits of government spending on social goods. Since this estimate affects both the numerator and denominator of the incidence ratio, it follows that fiscal incidence results based on actual post-fisc income carry a larger margin of error in measurement and should be treated with some caution.

As shown in Appendix Table A-1, actual post-fisc income is composed of private income, plus government transfer payments, plus the benefits of government purchases, minus taxes. Private income, in turn, includes three major components: private money income, such as wages, salaries and investment income; private non-money income, such as imputed rent from owner-occupied homes and the investment income of life insurance companies; and special adjustments primarily to include taxes that are paid, directly or indirectly, out of labour income.

Incidence Assumptions

TAXATION

Two major methodological advances were incorporated in our selection of tax shifting assumptions. First, we treated Canada as a small open economy, rather than the more common treatment as a closed economy, used especially in US studies. Second, we made an explicit adjustment for the indexing of government transfer payments to the consumer price index.

The small open economy assumption affects the pattern of incidence of various taxes through two basic channels: it prevents deviations between the domestic and the world rate of return on capital and it constrains the price that producers can change for internationally traded goods and services. The small open economy assumption affects the incidence of those taxes that would impose a differential burden on capital from average world rates or would affect producer prices. The burden of those tax components under perfect capital mobility and price-taking behaviour cannot be borne by either consumers or owners of capital and must be shifted to the immobile factors, labour and land. These conclusions have been used, where applicable, in our selection of the shifting assumptions.

The traditional approach to sales tax incidence ignored entirely the effect of transfer payments.[11] Browning (1978, 1985 and with Johnson, 1979) argued that government transfer payments to individuals affect the incidence of sales taxes because they do not bear the burden of such taxes. A reconciliation between the traditional approach and Browning's alternative has been recently proposed by Ruggeri (1993). Ruggeri shows that within the framework of differential tax incidence, where the standard of comparison is a proportional income tax applied to a comprehensive income base, transfers affect the pattern of incidence only to the extent they are indexed for increases in consumer prices. Moreover, the effect of indexing is properly captured by treating the actual degree of indexing as a negative tax. When measuring sales tax incidence, the amount of tax to be allocated is not the gross revenue collected, but the revenue net of the portion of transfers due to indexation. In our calculations each major government transfer to persons was adjusted by the estimated degree of indexing.[12] The indexing compensation was subtracted from each sales and excise tax assigned to consumers and from the transfers received by households, following the approach used in Ruggeri and Bluck (1990, 1992).

Details of the tax-shifting assumptions are found in the Appendix. Here we provide a summary for the major revenue sources.

Personal income taxes (PIT) were allocated in the traditional manner, i.e., to those paying them. For the average taxpayer in each of the 330 income-family type groups, the PIT payable was calculated on the basis of the rate structure, level of income, sources of income and special demographic features.

There is no agreement in the literature on who bears the burden of corporate income taxes (CIT).[13] At one extreme it is sometimes assumed that the taxes are fully shifted forward to consumers. At the other extreme, they are assumed not to be shifted at all. We used a compromise between the two extremes. First we allocated 50 percent of the CIT revenues (net of the petroleum and gas revenue tax which was treated as a commodity tax) to domestic consumers. From the other half we subtracted the share assumed to be borne by foreign recipients of Canadian dividends and the dividend tax credit, which is a repayment of corporate income tax imposed on cash dividends. For consistency, we did not subtract the dividend tax credit in the calculation of the PIT. The balance was allocated on the basis of capital gains, as the tax on retained earnings is not offset by a credit as in the case of dividends. The same approach was used for capital taxes.

In the case of sales taxes, the revenue net of indexing was allocated partly to consumers (direct component) and partly to adjusted factor income[14] (indirect component paid on business inputs). In a small open economy, where there is perfect mobility of capital and all goods and services are tradeable, indirect sales taxes on business inputs cannot be borne either by consumers or by capital owners. Therefore, they must be shifted to immobile factors, primarily labour. In our calculations, we assumed less than perfect capital mobility and allowed for some burden to be borne by capital owners. Excise tax revenue, also net of indexing, was allocated to the consumers of taxed items.

Payroll taxes were allocated entirely to labour income. This assumes that, over the long run, even the portion paid by the employee is ultimately reflected in lower wages. Both theoretical and empirical studies support this assumption, as indicated by Dahlby (1993).

As in the case of corporate taxes, there is no agreement on the incidence of real property taxes (see Aaron, 1975). We used a compromise approach. Property tax revenue was divided into three major components according to the source of the payment: residential homeowners, residential rental properties and commercial-industrial properties. The tax collected from homeowners was allocated entirely to them in accordance with the value of the property.[15]

The land component of the tax on residential rental properties and commercial-industrial properties was allocated to the owners (recipients of rental income in the case of residential rental properties and recipients of capital income for the rest) and the revenue from the tax on structures was allocated in equal proportion to consumers in general (renters in the case of residential rental properties) and recipients of capital income.[16]

GOVERNMENT EXPENDITURES

We divided government expenditures into transfer payments and purchases of goods and services. For both components of public spending, the benefits assigned to households were assumed to be equal to the cost incurred by the government. Therefore, what we allocated were expenditures on behalf of, rather than benefits received by, households. Tables A-6 to A-8 show the incidence assumptions that have been adopted for each type of expenditure in detail.

Equating the benefits with the costs of providing government services is an important assumption that has been used in all expenditure incidence studies. It implies that we are ignoring any external, or excess, benefits to other households or to society that may arise from either the public good or social good character of certain types of expenditures.

Transfers. According to Musgrave *et al.* (1974), transfer payments to persons can be treated as negative taxes and, therefore, can be allocated on the same basis. The same approach was employed by Gillespie, Dodge, Johnson, and Payette and Vaillancourt in their fiscal incidence studies of Canada, Ontario and Quebec. We divided transfers into direct transfers to persons, indirect transfers to persons and subsidies to business. For the first category we allocated only the net amount, after subtracting the component due to indexing.

We allocated all 12 direct transfers to persons, including federal and provincial refundable tax credits, to specific households in our micro database. Public and private pension income was allocated to pensioners. The interest on the portion of the public debt held by Canadians was allocated as income to recipients of interest income. However, it was not included in our estimates of the incidence of government transfers to households for two reasons. First, we omitted government borrowing from our estimates of tax incidence. Second, we are concerned with annual fiscal incidence; intertemporal financing decisions may be regarded as a separate issue.

In the case of indirect transfers to individuals, more general allocation procedures were required because we do not have specific data on the recipients of these programs. Grants to Aboriginal Peoples were allocated to households on the basis of the income profile of Indians living on reserves. Grants to charities and miscellaneous grants were allocated on the same basis as non-specific purchases of goods and services, discussed below. Grants and scholarships were allocated on the same basis as specific expenditures on postsecondary education, also discussed below. Finally, homebuyers' grants were allocated to recipients of non-farm imputed rent, which serves as a proxy for home ownership.

Agricultural subsidies were assumed to benefit farmers directly because, in a small open economy, farmers are price-takers. Those subsidies were allocated to farm households on the basis of net income from farming operations. Subsidies to health-care businesses were treated as benefits to the general public and allocated in the same manner as non-specific expenditures. Housing business subsidies were assumed to be passed forward to consumers of housing services by value of housing, split equally between homeowners and renters. All other subsidies to business were treated as negative excise taxes; they were assigned to households on the basis of their expenditures on total consumption.

Purchases. Government purchases of goods and services can be usefully divided into expenditures on social goods, which provide benefits to the entire community, and expenditures on goods that are substitutes for private consumption, which benefit specific households. The latter can be allocated to specific beneficiaries. Of the total government spending on purchases of goods and services, almost three-quarters (72 percent) was specifically allocated. The details of the allocation of specifically allocable expenditures are shown in the Appendix Table A-8.

In the case of education, public expenditures were allocated to families with children of school age, separated into elementary-secondary and postsecondary because the cost per student varies by level of education. Health-care expenditures were allocated to the representative member in each population group on the basis of age, utilization rate and income (see Marzouk 1991). Smeeding *et al.* (1993) point out that this is consistent with a "risk-related insurance premium approach," recognizing that the insurance benefit varies by age.[17]

There is no consensus in the literature on the appropriate allocation by household income of non-specific expenditures, such as protection of persons and property. We used two alternative assumptions in calculating the incidence of non-specific expenditures in order to provide an indication of the sensitivity of the estimates to this important assumption. First we estimated expenditure incidence by allocating all non-specific expenditures on the basis of total money income (referred to as case 1). Under this approach, non-specific expenditures are treated as complementary to private consumption. In case 2 we assigned non-specific expenditures on a per capita (i.e., an equal amount for each person in a household) basis, which is the assumption most consistent with their treatment as pure public goods.

The difficulties in allocating accurately the benefits of government purchases makes the measure of post-fisc income less precise than the widely-used measure of pre-fisc income plus transfers. This lack of precision, however, is more than offset by the comprehensiveness of the measure, which does not leave an important instrument of redistributional policy unaccounted for. For example, changes in provincial spending in health care and education could not be evaluated within the framework of partial post-fisc income.

Annual versus Lifetime Incidence

The traditional approach to the measurement of fiscal incidence is to group households into income classes in accordance with a measure of their annual income. Each class is then assigned a share of the total revenue raised by the government and a share of the benefits of the government expenditures in the same year. The ratio of the net benefits (burdens) received (borne) during a given year to the average annual income in each group provides a measure of fiscal incidence for that year.

During the past 20 years academic research has placed increasing emphasis on lifetime tax and fiscal incidence.[18] In contrast to the static framework of annual incidence, lifetime fiscal incidence evaluates the distributional impact of the fisc over an individual's lifetime, taking into account the dynamics that determine his/ her income path through time. Lifetime incidence measures the burden (benefits) of taxes (expenditures) as a ratio to lifetime income. Annual and lifetime incidence differ with respect to data requirements, incidence methodology and interpretation of results.[19]

It should be stressed that the two approaches are complementary and address different questions about the distributional impact of the fiscal system. Lifetime fiscal incidence depends on the profile of income through time, as well as lifetime income. Therefore, the correct measurement of lifetime incidence requires the separate calculation of annual incidence for each year of an individual's life.

How We Define the Rich, the Poor and the Middle Class

In order to facilitate the interpretation of our results for policy purposes, we aggregated census families, by family type, into upper, lower and middle income groups. This perspective relates the income classes to popular notions of socioeconomic characteristics. The approach raised a number of theoretical and methodological issues.

In deciding on the number of broad income classes to select, we were concerned that aggregation into three classes would make them too large for meaningful policy analysis. Therefore each of the above broad income classes were divided into two, yielding three income classes below and three above the median income. The income classes below the median are the poor, the low income class and lower-middle class; above the median are the upper-middle class, high income class, and the rich.

The importance attached to the poor in public policy discussion on redistribution requires that the "poor" income class be identified with an acceptable definition of poverty. A traditional notion of poverty is based on the amount of income required to provide "the basic necessities of life," such as food, shelter and clothing. This absolute measure of poverty is generally used to define needs tests for social assistance programs and underlies the US official poverty line. In practice, the absolute poverty concept cannot avoid value judgements, as the definition of necessities must generally take into account changing standards for participation in the normal life of the community (e.g., access to telephone, television, private transportation and cultural events).

An alternative approach, gaining increasing acceptance among policy analysts, measures poverty relative to the resources available to society. This makes an explicit value judgement by defining the poverty line as a percentage of the average income of households. Most European countries, the OECD and the researchers of the International Luxembourg Income Study define the poverty line as one-half of median income. Statistics Canada has adopted this approach for its Low Income Measures (LIM).[20] Since it is consistent with our interest in relative income redistribution, we define the "poor" as those households with income below 50 percent of the median income, adjusted for household size.

The other income classes are defined as follows. The "rich" are those households with income above three times the median.[21] Our definition of the rich differs from the popular view which includes only millionaires. It effectively includes those with incomes in the top 3.3 percent of households. The middle class is defined as households with income between 75 percent and 150 percent of the median, understanding that this selection, like any other, is arbitrary.[22] This broad middle-income class was divided into two by the median. The lower-middle class (those with income between the median and 75 percent of the median) and the upper-middle class (those with incomes between the median and 150 percent of the median). The remaining two classes are automatically determined. The low income class contains households with income between 50 percent and 75 percent of the median; the high income class contains households with income between 150 percent and 300 percent of the median.

To standardize the comparison among households of different sizes, it is necessary to take into account differences in consumption arising from economies of scale associated with additional members of a household. The use of equivalency scales in comparing the standard of living of different sizes of households is well accepted in the literature. There is little consensus, however, on the value of the scales.

Buhmann (1988) surveyed the equivalence scales used in a number of studies and found a range between 0.3 and 0.6, indicating that an additional household member adds 30 percent to 60 percent of the costs of the first member. Smeeding et al. (1993) allocated a weight of 1 to the first adult, 0.4 for each additional adult and 0.3 for each child. Statistics Canada, in its calculation of the Low Income Measure, uses a weight of 1.0 for the first member of a household, 0.4 for the second member and 0.3 for each additional member. We followed the Statistics Canada approach to allow a comparison with their results.

The equivalency scales are based on consumption of private goods and services, where economies of scale apply. The income concept to which the equivalency applies, therefore, should not include the benefits of government purchases. Smeeding et al. (1993) used disposable income, which takes into account both transfer payments received and income taxes paid. Statistics Canada, in its estimation of the low income cut-offs (LICO) and low income measures (LIM), uses family income before taxes. Again, in order to facilitate comparison of the results with widely used Canadian statistics, we used the latter.

The income thresholds for the household types by size are shown in Table 1-2. It should be remembered that these are 1986 values; in 1995 they would be about one-third higher. Table 1-3 shows the shares of population and households in each income class by the five selected household types. For example, the combined middle class accounted for 42.1 percent of the population and 36.9 percent of total households. These shares vary considerably among household types — in the case of two-income families, the middle class represents 50 percent of the population; for senior households, the corresponding share is 25.5 percent (Table 1-4).

TABLE 1-2: Income Threshholds for Major Income Classes by Household Size – 1986

	Poor	Low Income		Lower-Middle		Upper-Middle		High Income		Rich
Singles										
Family money income	less than 9,745	9,745	14,618	14,618	19,490	19,490	29,235	29,235	58,470	greater than 58,470
2 person households										
Family money income	less than 13,643	13,643	20,465	20,465	27,286	27,286	40,929	40,929	81,858	greater than 81,858
3 person households										
Family money income	less than 16,567	16,567	24,850	24,850	33,133	33,133	49,700	49,700	99,399	greater than 99,399
4 person households										
Family money income	less than 19,685	19,685	29,527	29,527	39,370	39,370	59,055	59,055	118,109	greater than 118,109
5+ person households										
Family money income	less than 22,706	22,706	34,059	34,059	45,412	45,412	68,118	68,118	136,235	greater than 136,235

Note: The values may be converted to 1995 dollars by increasing them by about one-third.

TABLE 1-3: Distribution of Population and Households by Income Class and Household Type

	Poor	Low Income	Lower-Middle	Upper-Middle	High Income	Rich	Total
Households							
Non-senior singles	7.5%	5.3%	3.5%	5.7%	4.5%	0.5%	26.9%
Single parents	2.5%	1.0%	0.8%	0.6%	0.2%	0.0%	5.2%
One-income families	3.1%	3.2%	3.5%	4.5%	2.9%	0.8%	18.1%
Two-income families	1.3%	3.0%	4.6%	9.2%	10.0%	1.5%	29.7%
Seniors	7.1%	6.0%	2.3%	2.2%	2.0%	0.4%	20.1%
Total households	21.6%	18.5%	14.7%	22.2%	19.6%	3.3%	100.0%
Population							
Non-senior singles	3.5%	2.4%	1.6%	2.6%	2.1%	0.2%	12.5%
Single parents	3.0%	1.3%	0.9%	0.7%	0.2%	0.0%	6.1%
One-income families	4.8%	5.2%	5.5%	6.2%	3.2%	1.0%	25.9%
Two-income families	2.1%	5.0%	7.4%	13.8%	12.3%	1.7%	42.4%
Seniors	4.1%	4.0%	1.7%	1.6%	1.5%	0.3%	13.2%
Total population	17.5%	17.9%	17.1%	25.0%	19.3%	3.3%	100.0%

TABLE 1-4: Shares of Population and Households by Income Class and Household Type

	Poor	Low Income	Lower-Middle	Upper-Middle	High Income	Rich	Total
Households							
Non-senior singles	27.9%	19.6%	13.1%	21.1%	16.7%	1.7%	100.0%
Single parents	48.6%	20.1%	15.1%	11.3%	4.5%	0.3%	100.0%
One-income families	17.1%	17.6%	19.5%	25.1%	16.1%	4.6%	100.0%
Two-income families	4.5%	10.1%	15.6%	30.8%	33.8%	5.2%	100.0%
Seniors	35.6%	29.9%	11.3%	11.2%	9.8%	2.2%	100.0%
Total households	21.6%	18.5%	14.7%	22.2%	19.6%	3.3%	100.0%
Population							
Non-senior singles	27.9%	19.6%	13.1%	21.1%	16.7%	1.7%	100.0%
Single parents	49.8%	20.9%	14.3%	10.8%	4.0%	0.3%	100.0%
One-income families	18.5%	20.0%	21.2%	24.0%	12.5%	3.7%	100.0%
Two-income families	5.0%	11.8%	17.4%	32.6%	29.0%	4.1%	100.0%
Seniors	30.9%	30.0%	13.1%	12.4%	11.0%	2.6%	100.0%
Total population	17.5%	17.9%	17.1%	25.0%	19.3%	3.3%	100.0%

NOTES

1. See R. Morissette, J. Myles and G. Picot (1994).
2. See, for example, William Robson, (1994).
3. See, for example, the report of the Ontario Fair Tax Commission, (1993).
4. The database is constructed as a partial simulated micro database from Statistics Canada's Survey of Consumer Finances. The tax data uses Revenue Canada's aggregated, *Taxation Statistics*, and the government spending data is from the Financial Management System of public accounts. Several other data sources are used for control totals and additional information. See pp. 13-14 for discussion of the micro database used in our study. Further details on the tax incidence analysis are provided in Horry, Palda and Walker (1994).
5. This leads to an underestimate of the degree of tax progressivity and inconsistent estimates of relative tax versus expenditure progressivity. See pp. 14-16 for more discussion.
6. See Musgrave, Musgrave and Bird (1987, pp. 233-37) for an explanation of these concepts.
7. An example is Horry and Walker's conclusion (1994, p. 154) that government spending on health care disproportionally benefits the rich. Their estimates of health-care benefits (p. 150) indicate that the average dollar benefit (absolute benefit) to the top decile of families was about double that of the bottom decile in 1990. However, the average post-fisc income of the top decile of families is 4.5 times that of the bottom decile and the average money income of the top decile is almost ten times that of the bottom decile. Therefore, health-care expenditures are much more equally distributed than pre- or post-fisc income and effectively redistribute income from upper to lower income families when financed by a distribution-neutral (proportional) tax.
8. For a description of the SPSD/M, see Bordt, Cameron, Gribble, Murphy, Rowe and Wolfson (1990).
9. Since the value of post-fisc income is responsive to the assumptions about the incidence of taxes and government expenditures, changes in those assumptions affect both the numerator and denominator of the effective tax and spending rates in a consistent manner.
10. For example, see Pechman and Okner (1980), and Vermaeten, Gillespie and Vermaeten (1994).
11. For example, see Pechman and Okner (1980).
12. The following transfers were indexed 100 percent: OAS, GIS, Family Allowance, Veterans' Pensions, UI and CPP. Workers' Compensation was indexed 90 percent and the Child Tax Credit and social assistance were indexed 75 percent. All other transfers were left unindexed.
13. See Harberger (1962); Musgrave, Musgrave and Bird (1987), pp. 263-265, 385-389; Baumol (1973); and Feldstein (1974).
14. Adjusted factor income was calculated by adding 100 percent of labour income, 50 percent of business income, and 25 percent of capital income. The different percentages

reflect differences in the mobility of labour and capital. Since the MST revenue allocated to factor income is only 22 percent of the total MST revenue and, since non-labour income is only 20 percent of total factor income in 1986, moderate changes in these percentages have little effect on the pattern of incidence.

15. This approach is theoretically consistent with the new view of property taxation. However, in our case it yields the same results as the traditional view because imputed rent, which represents a measure of housing services consumption, was allocated as a proportion of the value of the residential property.

16. Residential rental properties and commercial-industrial properties share a common feature: they serve to produce goods and services for sale to consumers. The issue then is whether the property tax on these structures should be treated as equivalent to an excise tax (traditional view) or as a corporate income tax (new view). As in the case of the CIT, we used a compromise approach between the two polar views. We assumed that neither the supply of structures nor the supply of capital is perfectly inelastic, and, therefore, allow for some forward shifting of the property tax on business structures.

17. Smeeding et al. (1993) allocated health-care expenditures (net of user fees) by age and gender in each age-gender cell. Their allocation of education expenditures was similar to ours. Our findings show that the combined effect of education and health-care spending is progressive (pro-poor); they found, similarly, that health care and education reinforces the redistributive impact of cash transfers.

18. Two studies that have analyzed lifetime tax incidence are Davies, St-Hilaire and Whalley (1984) for Canada and Fullerton and Rogers (1991) for the US Harding (1993) has estimated lifetime tax and transfer incidence for Australia, while Falkingham, Hills and Lessof (1993) have estimated the lifetime incidence of British social security transfers and their revenue sources. The first full study of lifetime fiscal incidence, that we are aware of, is Horry and Walker (1994) for Canada.

19. See Fullerton and Rogers (1991a and 1991b) for a comparison of lifetime with annual tax incidence.

20. See Statistics Canada, Catalogue 13-207, Annual, *Income Distributions by Size in Canada.*

21. The same definition was used by Wolfson et al. (1994).

22. Thurow (1984) used as borders 75 percent and 125 percent of the median, Blackburn and Bloom (1985) used 60 percent and 225 percent, and Wolfson et al. (1994) explored the implications of using 75 percent and 150 percent.

CHAPTER TWO

Fiscal Redistribution in Canada, 1986

This chapter presents estimates of the redistributional impact of the entire Canadian fiscal system. We recognize that government spending and taxation change the economic position of different household types (say singles versus couples) with the same income as well as that of individuals and households with different income. For that reason information on both vertical and horizontal dimensions of fiscal redistribution is presented. We also recognize that the three orders of government have different fiscal structures which may deliver different degrees of redistribution. Therefore, our results are presented for all three levels of governments combined and also separately for the federal, provincial and local governments.

VERTICAL DIMENSIONS

All Governments Combined

Our results are first summarized by using a global index of redistribution. This index, referred to as R_G, ranges in value between 0 and 2. It has a value of 1 if the fisc does not alter the distribution of income, is less than 1 if there is redistribution in favour of higher income classes and is greater than 1 if there is redistribution in favour of lower income classes. This global index is derived from the underlying local index, R_i, for each of the 22 income classes, where i is the representative member in a class. R_i is calculated, for each class, as the share of post-fisc income divided by the share of neutral-fisc income. This ratio indicates the proportional range in i's post-fisc income due to a particular budget item. The representative member in a class is not affected by the fisc if the value of R_i is 1; it gains (loses) if the value of R_i is greater (less) than 1.[1]

Table 2-1 shows two sets of results. In case 1, those government expenditures which could not be allocated directly to identifiable beneficiaries (such as protection of persons and property) are assigned to all households on the basis of the distribution of money income. In case 2, those expenditures are allocated on a per capita basis.

Our estimates of net redistribution include the $20.5 billion deficit incurred in 1986, as previously noted. The inclusion of the deficit, however, does not necessarily imply more or less redistribution. The effect of the deficit on fiscal redistribution depends on the incidence of the expenditure financed by the borrowing and on the assumptions adopted about the tax liability incurred.

Table 2-1 shows that, for all governments combined, the estimated value of R_G is greater than 1 under both cases. We conclude that, in 1986, *the Canadian fiscal system redistributed income from higher to lower income classes*. In both cases, *taxation was the most powerful vehicle of redistribution*. The relative redistributional impact of transfer payments and government purchases depends on the assumption used for the allocation of non-specific expenditures, but the differences between the two cases are moderate. When these expenditures are allocated to households on the basis of their money income (case 1), transfers are somewhat more redistributive than government purchases; the opposite result is obtained when the allocation is on a per-capita basis (case 2). We conclude that *the benefits of government purchases of goods and services delivered similar amounts of redistribution as direct transfers to persons*.

Our results do not lend support to the generally held view that taxation is roughly proportional[2] and that redistribution is largely delivered through transfer payments.

TABLE 2-1: Indices of Fiscal Redistribution in Canada, 1986
           All Governments

	R_G	
	Case 1	*Case 2*
Taxation	1.069	1.085
Spending		
Transfers	1.040	1.037
Purchases	1.030	1.046
Total	1.059	1.072
Net fiscal effect	1.122	1.149

Therefore, they put into question redistributional policies that call for increased reliance on the transfer system.

More details on fiscal redistribution are provided by calculating separately for each of 22 income classes the ratios of taxes paid, the benefits of government purchases received, and government transfer payments received to total post-fisc income. We present these detailed results for case 1 only for two reasons. First, the conclusions are very similar in both cases; presenting both sets of results would involve considerable repetition. Second, although both approaches are methodologically defensible, we find the arguments in favour of case 1 more convincing.

First, if public goods are "normal goods" and are not perfect substitutes for private goods, their demand should increase with the level of income. Second, a large share of non-specific expenditures is for national defence and protection of persons and property. Since real property, wealth and human capital are unequally distributed, one would expect that the benefits of protecting such assets would also be unequally distributed. If national defence and the police were financed through a private insurance scheme, the amounts of the premium would be expected to vary with the value of one's wealth, as is the case with the insurance of homes, motor vehicles, personal property and athletes.[3]

The tax and expenditure ratios by income class are shown in Figure 2-1 and the net gain or loss as a proportion of post-fisc income is presented in Figure 2-2.

It is evident that the tax system is progressive, as the tax ratio (which measures the effective tax rate for each income group) increases when income goes up. *Most of the tax progressivity, however, occurs at the lower end of the income scale.* In the income range from $15,000 to $40,000 the effective tax rate increases by 0.53 percentage points per $1,000 of additional income. The effective tax rate continues to increase over the upper income range, but much more slowly. Between incomes of $40,000 and $150,000 it increases by 0.11 percentage points per $1,000 of additional income. For income above $150,000 the tax system is practically proportional.

Redistribution in favour of lower income groups does not require steadily increasing effective tax rates; all it needs is for high income groups to pay above average effective tax rates. Despite the virtual constancy of the effective tax rate at the upper end of the income scale, there is considerable income redistribution from high to low income taxpayers because those with incomes above $36,000 pay above-average effective tax rates.

Combined government spending on transfers and on purchases of goods and services also follows a clearly progressive (pro-poor) pattern. The ratio of public expenditures to post-fisc income falls continuously when income rises. As in the case of taxation, most of the change takes place in the income range below $35,000.

FIGURE 2-1: Ratio of Taxes and Government Spending to Post-Fisc Income

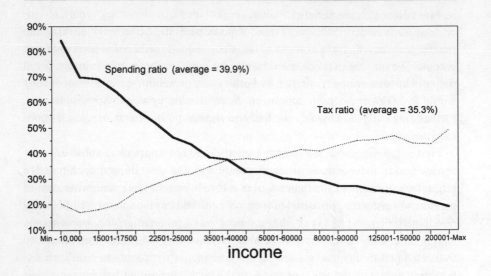

FIGURE 2-2: Net Fiscal Gain or Loss as a Percent of Post-Fisc Income

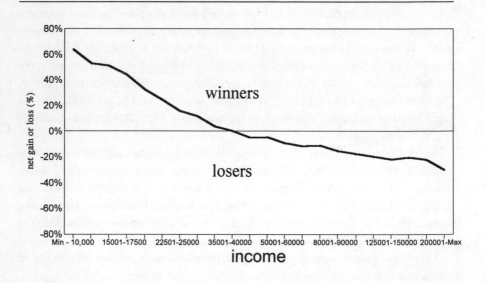

Above this income, the expenditure ratio falls very gradually. Households with income below $35,000 receive above average benefits and those above $35,000 receive below average benefits.

At income of $37,500, the tax and expenditure ratios intersect, marking the income level at which the amount of taxes paid equals the benefits received from government spending. Those with lower income receive a net gain from the fiscal system. As shown in Figure 2-2, *the gain is substantial for those with income below $20,000; it amounts to more than 50 percent of their post-fisc income. Those at the top end of the income scale (over $200,000) incur a loss that is equal to about 30 percent of their post-fisc income.*

Figure 2-3 compares the relative redistributional impact of government purchases and transfer payments. Both components of government spending are progressive (pro-poor) and their ratios to post-fisc income have somewhat similar patterns. Transfers to persons are relatively constant to income of $17,500, fall rapidly to income of $35,000, and gradually decline thereafter. Government purchases decline sharply to income of $17,500, continue to decline more gradually to income of $35,000, and are almost constant thereafter. The difference between these patterns of benefits is largely due to the income testing of some major transfers in order to target the benefits to low-income households.

FIGURE 2-3:   Effective Benefit Rates for Transfers and Purchases

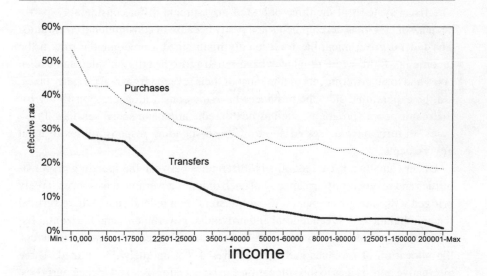

Government purchases are substantially higher in magnitude than transfers. Given their similar overall progressivity, this would suggest that they deliver a greater amount of redistribution. However, the amount of redistribution actually delivered, as shown in Table 2-1, is about the same as transfers. The reason for this result is that the amount of redistribution, measured as the change in the shares of post-fisc income brought about by the fiscal regime, is also affected by the income distribution of the population. The relative constancy of transfers below $17,500 means that the highest benefit ratio is received by a much larger share of the population at the lower income levels than in the case of purchases. In addition, transfers are more progressively distributed than purchases for income between $17,500 and $22,500 and above $35,000.

Part of the difference between the amounts of purchases and transfers allocated to households is due to our treatment of transfer indexing. As mentioned in Chapter 1, the portion of transfer payments associated with indexing for inflation was treated as a negative tax and, therefore, subtracted from gross transfer payments received and from taxes paid. When gross transfer payments are used, their ratio to post-fisc income is still much lower than the ratio for purchases in all income classes, with a maximum value of 37.7 percent, compared to 53.0 percent for purchases.

By Order of Government

The fiscal systems of the three orders of government differ considerably, partly because of historical developments and partly because of constitutional constraints. The federal government has traditionally maintained a predominant role in the income tax field, while provinces have relied more heavily on sales and excise taxes and local governments obtain most of their revenue from real property taxes. On the expenditure side, the provinces have the constitutional responsibility for the major people programs, such as health, education and social services. Provinces, in turn, have delegated some of those spending responsibilities to local governments.

Under Canadian fiscal federalism, differences between the spending responsibilities and revenue-raising capacity of each order of government have been largely bridged with intergovernmental fiscal transfers. In a federal state, where vertical fiscal imbalances between federal and provincial governments and horizontal fiscal imbalances among provinces are redressed through intergovernmental transfers, the allocation of revenues and expenditures is not uniquely determined. Three alternative approaches to this allocation can be used for fiscal incidence purposes.

Under one approach, revenues are assigned to the level of government which raises them and expenditures to the government that directly makes the spending.

In this case, the revenues of provincial and local governments fall short of their expenditures, while the federal government collects revenue in excess of its direct spending.[4]

Alternatively, one could assign revenue which is transferred to another order of government and the spending financed by that transfer to the donor government. In this case, provincial and local governments are largely administrative entities for the purpose of spending funds raised by the federal government. This assumes that a government is accountable only for the fiscal impact of the revenues it collects and the associated expenditures. Compared to the first approach, tax incidence estimates by order of government would remain unaffected, but expenditure incidence estimates would change.

Finally, one could assign to the recipient government that portion of revenue which is collected by a donor government to finance intergovernmental transfers, along with the associated spending. In this case, the donor government becomes partly a tax collector for revenue that is dedicated to other orders of government. Relative to the first approach, expenditure incidence estimates by order of government would remain unchanged, but tax incidence estimates would differ.

In this study we use the first approach, mainly because it accords most closely with the actual tax and expenditure policy responsibility exercised by the donor and recipient governments in Canada. This approach also allows comparability with earlier fiscal incidence studies.

The fiscal redistributional impact of the three orders of government is summarized in Table 2-2, which shows the value of the global redistributional index R_G.

TABLE 2-2: Indices of Fiscal Redistribution in Canada, 1986
By Order of Government

	R_G		
	Federal	Provincial	Local
Taxation	1.035	1.019	1.000
Expenditures			
Transfers	1.027	1.014	1.001
Purchases	1.003	1.028	1.003
Sub-total	1.029	1.039	1.004
Net fiscal effect	1.064	1.060	1.004

For the local governments, all components of the budget have a value of R_G close to 1. This indicates that *the fiscal system of local government has little impact on the distribution of income.*

The fiscal systems of the federal and provincial governments generate nearly equal degrees of redistribution. Our results for Canada do not support the generally-accepted view that the central government is the most powerful engine for delivering redistribution. They show that the federal and provincial governments differ with respect to the major instruments of redistribution, not to the degree of redistribution. At the federal level, redistribution is delivered almost entirely through taxation and transfer payments. At the provincial level, government purchases are the most powerful tool of redistribution, with taxation and transfers playing less significant roles.

Details on the pattern of fiscal gains and losses as a percentage of post-fisc income by income class and by order of government are shown in Figure 2-4.

The federal fiscal system generates a net loss of 3.2 percent of total post-fisc income because it has an excess of revenue over its spending (net of intergovernmental transfers). *Income of $30,000 separates the net fiscal winners from the losers.* As a proportion of post-fisc income, the gains by the lower income classes

FIGURE 2-4:   Net Fiscal Redistribution
Federal, Provincial and Local Government

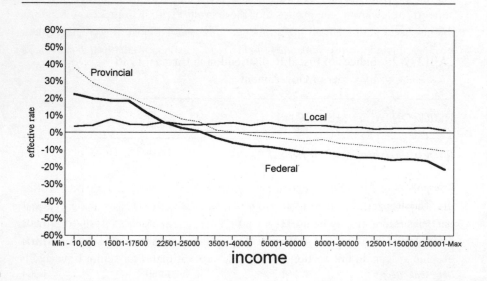

are almost equalled by the losses to the high income classes. *This redistributional impact is almost equally divided between taxation and expenditures.* Within expenditures, however, *transfers to persons are much more redistributive than purchases, which are virtually proportional.*

Provincial governments generate a net fiscal gain of 3.4 percent of post-fisc income because part of their expenditures are financed by transfers from the federal government. As a result, they are able to provide a larger gain to the lower income classes than the loss to the higher income classes. Annual income of about $38,000 separates the net fiscal winners from the losers. *Provincial expenditures are far more redistributive than taxes; purchases account for a larger amount of redistribution than transfers.*

Local governments generate a net fiscal gain for all income groups, averaging 4.5 percent of post-fisc income. The magnitude of this gain, relative to post-fisc income, fluctuates around the average for most of the income distribution and *shows a moderate downward trend only for income in excess of $80,000. Most of the small amount of redistribution originates from purchases, while taxation and transfers are roughly proportional.*

Relative to the other orders of government, the federal government delivers redistribution largely through the reduction of post-fisc income at the top of the income scale. This is largely due to the federal dominance of the personal income tax. In 1986 the fiscal impact of all governments combined, cost income classes above $100,000 on average approximately 23 percent of their post-fisc income; *nearly three-quarters of this loss was generated by the federal fiscal system.* Provincial governments, on the other hand, deliver redistribution largely by their support for lower income groups. For those groups with income below $20,000, the net fiscal gain from all governments represented almost 50 percent of their post-fisc income; *more than half of this gain was generated by the provincial fiscal system.*

HORIZONTAL DIMENSIONS

All Governments Combined

Tax policy, and to a larger extent policy determining transfer payments, is often directed at specific demographic groups, such as seniors, children and single parents. Therefore, it may be useful for policy formulation and analysis to provide estimates of the impact of government spending and taxation on selected demographic groups. In this section, we provide such estimates for senior households and four types of non-senior households: singles, single-parent families, one-income families with two parents and two-income families having two parents.

Figure 2-5 shows that, in 1986, the Canadian fiscal system created two clear winners and one clear loser among the five household types. *The big winners were households headed by a senior and to a smaller extent, single-parent families. The biggest losers were two-income families.*

The direction and magnitude of fiscal redistribution for each household type depends on its income distribution and average income, as well as the special provisions of the fiscal structure. In order to provide some insights into the interaction between the income distribution and the redistributional impact of the fiscal structure, we divided each household type into six policy-oriented income classes (see Chapter 1). Defining the six income classes separately for each household type adjusts for some of the key differences between them, such as average income, family size, number of dependents, number of income earners and age.

In the following discussion, our estimates of fiscal redistribution by household type and income groups are presented in absolute dollars in order to emphasize the size of the dollar flows between and within household types. We point out again that the net redistribution includes $20.5 billion of deficit finance. This

FIGURE 2-5:   Fiscal Redistribution by Demographic Group

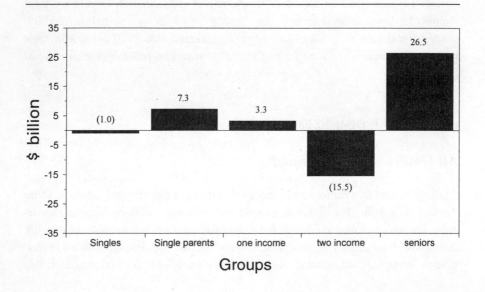

increases the size of absolute expenditure benefits relative to the tax burden. The results for each group on a per household basis are shown in Chapter 3. Table 2-3 presents the dollar amounts of redistribution for each of the five household types divided into the six income classes. The total amount of post-fisc income received by winners (the sum of the positive numbers in Table 2-3) is $58.4 billion. This amount includes the benefits of the $20.5 billion deficit incurred in 1986. *This is equivalent to 25 percent of total government spending. The poor received a net gain of $26.5 billion, or 45 percent of the total. The net redistribution to the poor income class represented 11 percent of total government spending.* The low income class gained $19.9 billion and the lower-middle class $7.3 billion.

With the exception of single-parent families and senior households, the winners are separated from the losers by the median income. For single-parent families, the redistributive impact is largely below the median, since there are very few members above the median income.[5] Senior households are all gainers with the exception of the rich, who experience a small loss.

With the actual 1986 deficit, non-senior singles as a whole were $1 billion worse off. There is near symmetry between the gains and losses by the top and the bottom half of the income distribution. Most of the redistribution among singles was from the high income class to the poor. The rich contributed one-sixth of the gain by those below the median and one-quarter of the gain by the poor. On a per household basis, the loss by the rich ($25,773) equalled the gain of four poor households ($6,287 each). Middle income singles were net losers ($2.4 billion or $3,861 per household).

One-income families gained $3.2 billion. With them the fisc played a large Robin Hood role: a gain of $5.2 billion by the poor was largely offset by a loss of $3.4 billion by the rich. The middle class was also a net gainer of $0.5 billion, or $1,872 per household. There was also redistribution within the middle class, with a $1.3 billion gain to the lower-middle class being offset by a loss of $0.8 billion by the upper-middle class.

Two-income families were the biggest losers in the redistribution process, with a net loss of $15.5 billion, or nearly $5,000 per household. There was only moderate redistribution within this household type. Although the rich lost $6.7 billion and the high income class an additional $12.4 billion, the poor gained only $1.9 billion. The gain by the poor is slightly larger than the gain by the lower-middle class ($1.7 billion). The middle class was a net loser ($1.4 billion) because the gain of $1.7 billion by the lower-middle class was more than offset by the loss of $3.1 billion by the upper-middle class. *Most of the fiscal redistribution that occurred in Canada in 1986 took the form of a transfer of purchasing power from upper-middle class and rich two-income couples to single-parent families and*

TABLE 2-3: Fiscal Redistribution by Household Type and Major Income Class

	Poor	Low Income	Lower-Middle	Upper-Middle	High Income	Rich	Total
				Millions of Dollars			
Non-senior singles	4,935	2,210	105	(2,462)	(4,660)	(1,235)	(1,105)
Single parents	5,016	1,753	535	5	(7)	(27)	7,275
One-income families	5,167	3,349	1,318	(805)	(2,417)	(3,372)	3,240
Two-income families	1,935	3,148	1,671	(3,119)	(12,424)	(6,674)	(15,463)
Seniors	9,435	9,432	3,711	3,137	1,552	(687)	26,580
Total	26,488	19,892	7,340	(3,245)	(17,955)	(11,994)	20,526
	Poor	Low Income	Lower-Middle	Upper-Middle	High Income	Rich	Net
				Dollars Per Household			
Non-senior singles	6,287	4,010	286	(4,147)	(9,918)	(25,773)	(393)
Single parents	19,023	16,069	6,522	74	(275)	(18,273)	13,415
One-income families	16,016	10,071	3,572	(1,700)	(7,952)	(38,508)	1,715
Two-income families	13,717	10,046	3,440	(3,258)	(11,840)	(41,383)	(4,975)
Seniors	12,629	15,015	15,683	13,352	7,536	(14,862)	12,663
Average	11,723	10,284	4,763	(1,398)	(8,743)	(34,823)	1,963

seniors. This transfer amounted to $22.2 billion of the $37.9 billion redistributed net of the deficit.

Single-parent families gained $7.3 billion. Two-thirds of this gain was received by the poor. There was virtually no redistribution within this household type. The gain per household of the poor and low income single-parent families was the largest of all household types. The gain of $16,069 per low income single-parent family exceeded that of the poor in every other family type.

Households headed by a senior gained in all income groups except the rich. The total gain amounted to $26.6 billion. Middle income seniors gained almost three-quarters ($6.8 billion) of the gain by the poor ($9.4 billion). Moreover, the per household gain of seniors in the low, lower-middle and upper-middle income classes exceeded that of poor seniors. The $7,536 per household gain by high income seniors exceeded the gain per household of the low income classes in all other family types.

Our results do not support the view that the middle class bears the heaviest burden of redistribution. In 1986 the lower-middle class received a net fiscal gain in all five demographic groups. Even within the upper-middle class, there were substantial gains by senior households. The net loss for the entire class was a moderate $3.2 billion, or $1,398 per household.

The Canadian fiscal system does have some Robin Hood aspects, as there is net redistribution from the rich to the poor. However, *there were considerable gains also for the low income and lower-middle classes. These two income classes combined gained slightly more ($27.2 billion) than the poor ($26.5 billion).* Redistribution involved primarily a transfer of resources from the top two income classes of singles, one- and two-income families to seniors and families in the poor and low income classes.

These results raise some important issues. How do we justify the large gains from fiscal redistribution to income classes not considered poor? Is this redistribution within classes other than the poor and the rich the outcome of deliberate social policy design or the unexpected result of uncoordinated policies? Proposals to reform the Canadian fiscal system should address these questions.

Another important and closely related issue arises from the results shown in Table 2-3. Redistribution has clearly an intergenerational dimension. Although a detailed evaluation of the intergenerational implications of Canada's fiscal structure must await a full lifetime fiscal incidence study, our results provide some general indications. If single-parent families are ignored, the remaining household types can be ordered according to increasing age as follows: singles, couples, seniors.

Our results show that the youngest group, singles, incurs a small fiscal loss. As they form families, especially two-income families, they become severely penalized by the fiscal system. However, they recover their losses after they retire from the labour force at 65 years of age. If one viewed the fiscal system strictly from an efficiency perspective, one might question the merits of a fiscal structure that penalizes households during their labour attachment years, when they make labour supply decisions, and rewards them when they no longer have an attachment to the labour force.

More detailed information which will help evaluate these issues is contained in Chapter 3. First, however, we will briefly discuss the federal-provincial-local dimensions of interhousehold fiscal redistribution.

By Order of Government

Table 2-4 shows that, by treating intergovernment fiscal transfers as expenditures of the recipient government, the federal government collected nearly $15 billion revenue in excess of its direct spending in 1986. This translates into a $15 billion net fiscal loss to households. The opposite is true for the other two orders of government. That relationship, however, holds strictly only for non-senior singles and one-income couples. In both of those family types, the fiscal loss at the federal level is more or less offset by gains at the provincial and local level.

Single-parent families receive net gains from all three orders of government, but the share due to the federal fiscal system is very small. Two-income couples, on the other hand, receive net fiscal benefits only from the local fiscal system, while incurring large losses from the fiscal systems of the federal and provincial

TABLE 2-4: Fiscal Redistribution by Demographic Group and Order of Government

| | $ Million | | | |
	Federal	Provincial	Local	Total
Non-senior singles	(5,473)	3,739	628	(1,105)
Non-senior single parents	677	3,756	2,842	7,275
Non-senior one-income couples	(4,949)	3,579	4,610	3,240
Non-senior two-income couples	(20,770)	(6,487)	11,795	(15,463)
Seniors	15,805	10,649	127	26,580
Total	(14,710)	15,235	20,001	20,526

governments, especially from the former. At the local level they benefit from subsidized primary and secondary education; at the federal and provincial level they make the largest contribution to government revenue, particularly personal income taxes. The details on the particular taxes and expenditure programs are presented in the next chapter.

NOTES

1. The local redistributional measure, R_i, is based on the relative share adjustment (RSA) introduced by Baum (1987). Ruggeri, Van Wart and Cassady (1992) have shown how the RSA can be aggregated into the global index of redistribution, R_G. The global index is calculated as the weighted sum of the local indices, where the weights are the relative local shares of neutral-fisc income. R_G has been previously proposed as a global index of redistribution by Pfähler (1987).

   The local RSA is closely related to the effective tax (or benefit) rate. In the case of taxation, the local index is calculated as

$$RSA_i = \frac{1-t_i}{1-t}$$

   where t is the overall average tax rate and t_i is the effective tax rate of income class i. For government purchases or transfer payments, the minus sign in the numerator and denominator becomes a plus. There is additional discussion on the measure of incidence in the Appendix.

2. For the traditional proportional view, see Vermaeten, Gillespie and Vermaeten (1994). These results are compared with our detailed results for tax incidence in the same volume, Ruggeri, Van Wart and Howard (1994).

3. For a review of alternative approaches to the allocation of the benefit of government purchases, see the Aaron and McGuire (1970, 1975) and their debate with Brennan (1976).

4. This is the approach used in Statistics Canada's National Income and Expenditures Accounts (NIA). The Financial Management System (FMS) accounts, also published by Statistics Canada, allocate both the revenue and expenditure for specific purpose transfers to the donor government, but treat the general purpose transfers in the same way as the NIA. This is a mix of the first approach and second approach below.

5. Because of the relatively small number of observations in the classes above the median, it may be advisable to ignore the results for single-parent families in those income classes.

CHAPTER THREE

Fiscal Redistribution in Canada: Selected Programs

This chapter provides more details on the effectiveness of specific government programs as vehicles of redistribution. A brief look at taxation is followed by a review of the major functional categories of government purchases and, finally, an analysis of government transfer payments to persons and to business.

TAXATION

It was shown in Chapter 2 that in 1986 the Canadian tax system generated a progressive pattern of incidence overall and provided considerable redistribution between income classes. *Tax redistribution from higher to lower income groups is due entirely to the personal income tax.* As shown in Figure 3-1, the effective PIT rate (PIT revenue as a percentage of post-fisc income) increases steadily, from 0.3 percent for the lowest income group (up to $10,000) to 35.0 percent for the group with income over $200,000. The income group $40,000 to $45,000 bears the average burden (14.1 percent). By itself, the PIT redistributes income from those with income above $42,500 to those with income below that level.

All other taxes combined exhibit an inverted U-shaped pattern of incidence. They generate redistribution from the middle class, broadly defined, to both the low and high income classes. Canadians with income from $20,000 to $75,000 bear a tax burden from non-PIT taxes in excess of the average rate of 21.2 percent. In addition, the effective tax rate for non-PIT taxes of the top income classes is lower than that of the bottom income classes. *The overall regressivity of non-PIT taxes, therefore, arises more from well-to-do Canadians paying too little than from the poor paying too much.* The results could be interpreted as indicating that

FIGURE 3-1: Personal Income Tax versus Other Taxes
Ratio to Post-Fisc Income

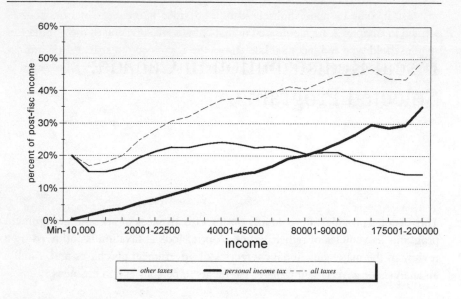

a portion of the progressivity of the PIT does not generate positive redistribution of income from rich to poor; it simply offsets the negative (pro-rich) redistribution generated by the non-PIT taxes.

The lowest income households benefit from below-average effective tax rates for both the PIT and all other combined taxes, although the benefit from the PIT is substantially higher. For households with income between $20,000 and $35,000, low PIT rates were associated with above-average non-PIT tax rates, generating a total tax burden close to the average of 35.3 percent. Those with income between $35,000 and $45,000 paid below-average to average PIT rates and above average non-PIT rates, for a combined tax burden above the average. Households with income between $45,000 and $70,000 bore above average tax rates for both the PIT and all other taxes. For those with income above $70,000, relatively high PIT rates were moderated by below-average non-PIT tax rates.

The low effective rates for taxes other than the PIT paid by low income households can be attributed to three factors. First, lower income households spend a considerably higher proportion of their income on basic necessities, such as food, shelter and heating, which are exempt from retail sales taxes. Second, transfer payments make up a relatively large proportion of the income of the lowest income classes. Most of the major transfers are indexed for increases in the price of consumer goods, therefore, they bear little of the burden of sales and excise taxes. Finally, transfers incur no payroll taxes.

Table 3-1 provides a breakdown of the effective PIT and non-PIT tax rates on post-fisc income by major household types divided into the six income classes defined in Chapter 2. As mentioned in that chapter, the division of the population by household type and income class shows the combined redistributional impact of a number of factors. These include the special treatment of selected households

TABLE 3-1: Effective Tax Rates by Household Type

	Single	Total SPF	Total 1 Income	Total 2 Income	Total Seniors	Combined Total
	%	%	%	%	%	%
Poor						
Personal income tax	0.7	0.2	1.0	1.3	0.0	0.5
Other taxes	31.8	11.1	14.8	18.3	7.7	16.3
All taxes	32.5	11.3	15.7	19.7	7.7	16.8
Low income						
Personal income tax	6.8	3.7	5.9	6.1	1.0	4.5
Other taxes	29.8	16.8	20.1	21.3	6.8	17.9
All taxes	36.6	20.5	26.0	27.4	7.8	22.4
Lower-middle						
Personal income tax	11.8	8.2	10.1	10.4	4.1	9.4
Other taxes	32.7	23.2	23.1	24.0	9.7	22.6
All taxes	44.5	31.3	33.1	34.4	13.8	32.0
Upper-middle						
Personal income tax	14.9	12.2	13.7	15.2	8.0	13.9
Other taxes	33.1	23.8	23.7	24.2	10.0	24.0
All taxes	48.0	36.0	37.3	39.4	18.0	37.9
High income						
Personal income tax	19.1	15.3	17.5	20.6	12.8	18.9
Other taxes	29.0	24.0	21.8	22.9	12.9	22.6
All taxes	48.0	39.3	39.3	43.5	25.7	41.5
Rich						
Personal income tax	26.6	37.8	28.5	31.0	25.8	29.2
Other taxes	21.2	21.5	16.7	17.2	15.8	17.3
All taxes	47.8	59.3	45.2	48.3	41.6	46.5
All income classes						
Personal income tax	13.5	6.0	14.0	17.9	7.0	14.1
Other taxes	30.3	17.7	20.9	22.5	9.9	21.2
All taxes	43.9	23.7	34.9	40.3	17.0	35.3

(for example, the age credit for seniors, the equivalent to married credit for the first child of a single parent, the deduction of child care expenses by single parents and two-income couples). They also include the differences in the average income and income distribution among the five household types and differences in the components of that income. Not all income is taxed equally; for example, capital gains in 1986 were taxed at one-half of the rate on employment income and dividends were eligible for a combined federal-provincial tax credit of 35 percent of the tax payable on the grossed-up amount.

For the combined household types in Table 3-1, the effective tax rate on the rich is 2.8 times that for the poor and only 23 percent higher than that of the upper middle class. For non-PIT taxes, the effective rate paid by the rich (17.3 percent) was slightly higher than the rate paid by the poor (16.3 percent), but lower than the rate paid by all other income classes.

The largest share of tax revenue (35.2 percent) originated from the high income class; the upper middle class contributed 26.2 percent and the rich 14.7 percent. Tables 3-1 and 3-2 shed some light on the tax burden borne by the middle class. This class paid 37.9 percent of taxes, slightly more than its share of households (36.9 percent) but less than its share of the population (42.1 percent). The middle class paid below-average effective PIT rates; its tax burden comes largely from non-PIT taxes.

Singles paid the highest effective tax rate among family types in 1986, 43.9 percent of post-fisc income. Over two-thirds of that burden was imposed by non-PIT taxes. Among these other taxes, the largest contributors to this burden were payroll taxes (7.2 percent), general sales taxes (6.7 percent), excise taxes (5.6 percent) and real property taxes (4.5 percent). *Non-PIT taxes imposed a heavier burden than the PIT on singles in all broad income classes except the rich.* Moreover, *the burden of non-PIT taxes is higher for singles than for all other household types in all income classes.* These results may be attributable to the high rate of consumption out of income by singles, who are younger on average than the general population and, therefore, may have lower current savings in anticipation of higher future earnings.

The second highest effective tax rate among household types is borne by households headed by two income earners, which paid 40.3 percent of post-fisc income in taxes in 1986. *The PIT is a much more significant burden for this group, accounting for almost 45 percent of the total tax burden.* Moreover, *for the rich, the effective PIT rate (31.0 percent) was much higher than the effective rate of non-PIT taxes (17.2 percent).* Among the non-PIT taxes, the most significant were payroll taxes (6.0 percent) and general sales taxes (5.0 percent).

One-income families paid an effective tax rate (34.9 percent) slightly lower than the average (35.3 percent). Like two-income families, the PIT is a significant

TABLE 3-2: Tax Burden by Household Type

	Single	Total SPF	Total 1 Income	Total 2 Income	Total Seniors	Combined Total
Poor						
Millions of dollars	3,085	730	1,360	836	984	6,996
Dollars per household	3,931	2,770	4,215	5,929	1,317	3,096
Low income						
Millions of dollars	3,491	802	3,261	3,469	1,272	12,295
Dollars per household	6,335	7,348	9,807	11,069	2,025	6,356
Lower-middle						
Millions of dollars	3,495	947	5,373	7,492	1,265	18,572
Dollars per household	9,509	11,553	14,567	15,421	5,344	12,053
Upper-middle						
Millions of dollars	8,058	1,064	9,157	20,704	2,063	41,047
Dollars per household	13,575	17,298	19,323	21,623	8,782	17,681
High income						
Millions of dollars	10,048	649	8,530	32,326	3,858	55,410
Dollars per household	21,388	26,408	28,060	30,808	18,726	26,982
Rich						
Millions of dollars	2,256	106	6,547	11,677	2,604	23,191
Dollars per household	47,106	73,269	74,777	72,398	56,314	67,330
All income classes						
Millions of dollars	30,435	4,298	34,229	76,503	12,046	157,510
Dollars per household	10,812	7,926	18,115	24,612	5,738	15,067

burden, accounting for over 40 percent of total taxes paid. The effective PIT rate was higher than that of non-PIT taxes only for the rich. The major components of non-PIT taxes for these households were payroll taxes (5.6 percent), general sales taxes (4.2 percent) and property taxes (3.6 percent).

Single parents bore an effective tax burden (23.7 percent) that is only two-thirds of the average. Like singles, *most of this burden is generated by non-PIT taxes; the effective rate of non-PIT taxes is three times that of the PIT.*[1] The major components of these taxes are payroll taxes (4.5 percent), general sales taxes (3.5 percent) and excise taxes (3.0 percent).

A special characteristic of single-parent households is the large proportion of income received from government transfers. Transfers do not incur any payroll tax and very little consumption taxes. As income increases, however, the share from wages grows. This tends to make the payroll taxes progressive and reduces the degree of regressivity of sales taxes for this household type. This is reflected in the increase in the non-PIT tax rate from the upper-middle to the rich income class.

Seniors bear the lowest tax burden of all household types. At 17.0 percent, the effective rate is less than half of the average in 1986. This tax burden is more evenly distributed between the PIT (7.0 percent) and other taxes (9.9 percent). *Although the average income of seniors is substantially higher than that of singles, their effective PIT rate is almost half that of singles.* This result highlights the special income tax treatment of seniors. A larger proportion of their income is non-taxable (GIS, Spouse's Allowance and provincial GIS supplements) and they benefit from special non-refundable credits for age and pension income.[2]

The low PIT burden on seniors is paralleled by a relatively even lower burden of all other taxes combined (47 percent of the average compared to 50 percent of the average for the PIT). This somewhat surprising result is due to two major factors. First, seniors do not incur payroll taxes, as they are generally out of the labour force (the effective payroll tax rate on seniors is less than 1 percent). Second, and *contrary to conventional wisdom, seniors do not bear a disproportionate share of sales taxes.*

In our estimates, the effective sales tax rate for seniors was about half of the average, while the effective excise tax rate was even less than half of the average. At retirement most seniors already own their furniture and appliances, and many fully own their homes. Their expenses, on average, involve a large proportion of non-taxed goods and expenditures on travel abroad.[3] Also, and most importantly, like the single-parent families, seniors receive a larger proportion of their income from transfer payments, most of which are fully indexed for consumer price increases (such as OAS, GIS, Spouse's Allowance and CPP/QPP benefits). As mentioned in Chapter 1, the inflation indexing of transfers offsets the burden of sales taxes. This factor largely accounts for a peculiar feature of the seniors: the non-PIT taxes have a progressive pattern of incidence, with the effective rate increasing from 7.7 percent for the poor to 15.8 percent for the rich.

Table 3-2 presents some information on the magnitude of the total tax burden on the household types by income class for 1986. Nearly 50 percent of tax revenue was collected from two-income families, an additional 22 percent was collected from one-income families, and 19 percent from singles. Families headed by seniors and single parents contributed 8 percent and 3 percent, respectively, although they accounted for 13.2 percent and 6.1 percent of the population, 20.1 percent and 5.2 percent of households, and 15.9 percent and 4.1 percent of post-fisc income.

Table 3-2 also shows that there are large variations in the tax burden per household, both within and between household types. Looking at all income classes together, we notice that *only non-senior households headed by two parents pay above average taxes per household.* In 1986, two-income families paid nearly two-thirds more than the average of $15,067 and one-income families paid 20 percent more than the average. Households headed by a senior paid 38 percent of the average. As previously noted, this is slightly more than half of what singles pay, although seniors have a higher average income.

Examining the household types by income class, Table 3-2 shows that households with below-median income paid below-average taxes per household, with the exception of lower-middle, two-income families. Upper middle class singles and seniors also paid below-average taxes per household.

Redistributional Significance of a Progressive PIT

To conclude the examination of the tax system, we reiterate that the only reason the tax system generates substantial redistribution is a personal income tax that has a progressive rate structure and accounts for a large share of government revenue.

There has been considerable discussion in recent years about the possibility of replacing the existing progressive rate structure of the PIT with a flat rate income tax. Two versions of the flat tax have been proposed. Under the first option, there would be a single tax rate applied to a comprehensive income concept (deductions, credits and exemptions would be eliminated or strictly limited), but there would also be personal exemptions.[4] Such a flat rate PIT would remain progressive, as effective rates would continue to increase with income; its degree of progressivity would be determined by the size of the personal exemptions. However, if the PIT burden on low income taxpayers is constant, a revenue-neutral shift from the current multi-rate to a flat rate structure with personal exemptions would likely involve a shift of the tax burden from high to middle income taxpayers. The extent of this shift would depend on the distribution of the tax preferences that would be eliminated.

The second option involves a single tax rate without exemptions. This option would eliminate progressivity entirely; it would reduce the PIT to a proportional tax on comprehensive income. Since all other taxes combined do not exhibit any progressivity, as they redistribute income from the middle class to the rich and the poor, such a flat rate income tax would effectively neutralize the tax system as an instrument of redistribution. It would also reduce the degree of overall redistribution by the Canadian fiscal system to less than half of its level in 1986.

GOVERNMENT SPENDING

In Chapter 2 government spending was also found to have a progressive (pro-poor) pattern of incidence. Additional details on the distribution of government expenditures by household type and major income classes are shown in Table 3-3.

The progressive pattern of government spending is confirmed by the declining share of government expenditures as we move to higher income classes. In 1986,

TABLE 3-3: Total Government Expenditures by Family Type
Combined all Government Transfers and Purchases

	Single	Total SPF	Total 1 Income	Total 2 Income	Total Seniors	Combined Total
Poor						
Millions of dollars	8,037	5,766	6,530	2,769	10,400	33,503
Dollars per household	10,239	21,866	20,240	19,632	13,921	14,828
Percent of income	84.7%	89.5%	75.6%	65.1%	81.4%	80.5%
Low income						
Millions of dollars	5,713	2,564	6,614	6,612	10,685	32,188
Dollars per household	10,365	23,501	19,888	21,100	17,010	16,640
Percent of income	59.8%	65.5%	52.7%	52.2%	65.7%	58.6%
Lower-middle						
Millions of dollars	3,608	1,487	6,695	9,156	4,967	25,913
Dollars per household	9,815	18,141	18,149	18,847	20,990	16,817
Percent of income	45.9%	49.2%	41.3%	42.0%	54.2%	44.6%
Upper-middle						
Millions of dollars	5,609	1,073	8,356	4,441	5,191	37,801
Dollars per household	9,449	17,437	17,633	4,638	22,094	16,283
Percent of income	33.4%	36.3%	34.1%	8.5%	45.2%	34.9%
High income						
Millions of dollars	5,401	645	6,116	19,886	5,398	37,447
Dollars per household	11,497	26,244	20,119	18,953	26,204	18,235
Percent of income	25.8%	39.0%	28.2%	26.8%	36.0%	28.0%
Rich						
Millions of dollars	1,024	80	3,177	4,998	1,912	11,192
Dollars per household	21,385	55,165	36,289	30,988	41,347	32,493
Percent of income	21.7%	44.6%	21.9%	20.7%	30.6%	22.5%
All income classes						
Millions of dollars	29,393	11,614	37,488	60,994	38,554	178,042
Dollars per household	10,441	21,417	19,840	19,623	18,367	17,031
Percent of income	42.4%	63.9%	38.2%	32.1%	54.3%	39.9%

government spending represented 80.5 percent of post-fisc income for the poor, 44.5 percent for the lower middle class and 22.5 percent for the rich. In dollar amounts, the largest beneficiaries were the upper middle class with $37.8 billion or 21.2 percent of the total and the high income class with $37.4 billion or 21.0 percent. The middle class as a whole received $63.7 billion or 35.8 percent of the total, slightly less than its share of households (36.9 percent) and of tax revenue (37.9 percent). On a per household basis, the largest benefits went to the rich. At $32,493 they were 90.8 percent higher than the average. The low- to upper-middle income classes received about the same amounts per household, while the poor received somewhat less ($14,828) and the high income class somewhat more ($18,235).

The next sections provide greater detail on the components of total government spending.

Government Purchases

Table 3-4 shows that government purchases have a pattern of incidence that is not as progressive as that of total government spending. This confirms the detailed incidence by income class shown in Table 2-3. Government purchases represent 51.9 percent of post-fisc income for the poor, 31.8 percent for the lower middle class and 19.5 percent for the rich. The largest share of total benefits was received by the high income class (23.6 percent), followed closely by the upper middle class (22.3 percent). The middle class as a whole received 36.4 percent, nearly equal to its share of households. On a per household basis, the rich received over twice the average, while the poor received three-quarters of the average.

In order to facilitate policy interpretation, we divided government purchases into four major categories and present the results by family type and major income class. The first category contains spending on general government and protection of persons and property. We call this category public goods, as they involve the portion of government spending that is not specifically allocated to identifiable beneficiaries. The second category includes government spending on health care, education, recreation and culture, and housing for low income Canadians. This category, which is almost identical to Kuznets' definition of government consumption, we call social goods because it involves the subsidization of goods and services which society wants to be consumed by all in amounts greater than under private market allocation. The third category involves government expenditures which may be considered intermediate inputs into private activity. It includes government spending on transportation and communications, resource conservation, industrial development, regional planning and development, and the environment.

TABLE 3-4:   Total Government Purchases by Family Type

	Single	Total SPF	Total 1 Income	Total 2 Income	Total Seniors	Combined Total
Poor						
Millions of dollars	5,964	4,022	4,409	2,288	4,907	21,590
Dollars per household	7,598	15,253	13,666	16,218	6,568	9,556
Percent of income	62.8%	62.4%	51.0%	53.8%	38.4%	51.9%
Low income						
Millions of dollars	4,018	1,901	4,577	5,243	4,880	20,619
Dollars per household	7,290	17,428	13,762	16,730	7,769	10,659
Percent of income	42.1%	48.6%	36.5%	41.4%	30.0%	37.5%
Lower-middle						
Millions of dollars	2,635	1,132	4,942	7,424	2,305	18,437
Dollars per household	7,168	13,805	13,397	15,281	9,740	11,965
Percent of income	33.5%	37.4%	30.5%	34.1%	25.1%	31.8%
Upper-middle						
Millions of dollars	4,482	830	6,359	1,779	2,456	29,038
Dollars per household	7,551	13,498	13,419	1,858	10,455	12,508
Percent of income	26.7%	28.1%	25.9%	3.4%	21.4%	26.8%
High income						
Millions of dollars	4,626	566	4,860	17,644	3,052	30,748
Dollars per household	9,848	23,027	15,987	16,816	14,815	14,973
Percent of income	22.1%	34.3%	22.4%	23.7%	20.3%	23.0%
Rich						
Millions of dollars	913	51	2,788	4,725	1,258	9,735
Dollars per household	19,071	35,258	31,847	29,293	27,194	28,264
Percent of income	19.3%	28.5%	19.3%	19.5%	20.1%	19.5%
All income classes						
Millions of dollars	22,639	8,502	27,935	52,232	18,858	130,167
Dollars per household	8,042	15,678	14,784	16,804	8,984	12,451
Percent of income	32.6%	46.8%	28.5%	27.5%	26.6%	29.2%

The fourth, and relatively small, category contains miscellaneous expenditures which do not fit closely into the first three.[5]

Table 3-5 shows that government expenditures on general government and protection of persons and property has a regressive (pro-rich) pattern of incidence when expressed as a proportion of post-fisc income. The increasing ratio of expenditures on public goods as we move to higher income classes results from the allocation of those expenditures on the basis of money income. Money income constitutes an increasing share of post-fisc income because of the pro-poor pattern

TABLE 3-5: Public Goods

	Singles	Single Parents	One-Income Families	Two-Income Families	Seniors	Total
Poor						
Millions of dollars	398	201	351	173	592	1,716
Dollars per household	508	763	1,089	1,229	792	760
Percent of income	4.2%	3.1%	4.1%	4.1%	4.6%	4.1%
Low income						
Millions of dollars	544	170	676	667	815	2,872
Dollars per household	987	1,561	2,034	2,127	1,297	1,485
Percent of income	5.7%	4.4%	5.4%	5.3%	5.0%	5.2%
Lower-middle						
Millions of dollars	517	168	991	1,305	505	3,487
Dollars per household	1,406	2,054	2,686	2,687	2,135	2,263
Percent of income	6.6%	5.6%	6.1%	6.0%	5.5%	6.0%
Upper-middle						
Millions of dollars	1,198	188	1,622	3,438	678	7,124
Dollars per household	2,018	3,053	3,423	3,591	2,888	3,069
Percent of income	7.1%	6.4%	6.6%	6.5%	5.9%	6.6%
High income						
Millions of dollars	1,551	103	1,503	5,253	954	9,363
Dollars per household	3,301	4,175	4,943	5,006	4,630	4,559
Percent of income	7.4%	6.2%	6.9%	7.1%	6.4%	7.0%
Rich						
Millions of dollars	357	14	1,068	1,822	450	3,711
Dollars per household	7,446	9,602	12,201	11,298	9,733	10,775
Percent of income	7.6%	7.8%	7.4%	7.5%	7.2%	7.4%
All income classes						
Millions of dollars	4,564	844	6,211	12,659	3,994	28,273
Dollars per household	1,621	1,557	3,287	4,073	1,903	2,704
Percent of income	6.6%	4.6%	6.3%	6.7%	5.6%	6.3%

of total fiscal incidence. The largest single beneficiary of public goods is the high income class, with one-third of the total. The middle class as a whole received 37.5 percent, which is more than its share of households. On a per household basis, combined households with income above the median received above-average benefits, both in dollars per household and as a share of post-fisc income.

Among household types, two-income families received the largest benefits from expenditures on public goods, with a share of 44.8 percent, followed by one-income families (22.0 percent) and non-senior singles (16.1 percent). This represented approximately 6.5 percent of post-fisc income for these three family types, slightly above the average. Seniors and single-parent families received below-average benefits as a proportion of post-fisc income (5.6 percent and 4.6 percent, respectively). Dollars per household varied widely by household type. Two-income families received $4,073 on average, which is 2.6 times that of single-parent families ($1,557).

Government expenditures on social goods (health care, education, recreation and culture, and social housing) have a decidedly progressive (pro-poor) pattern of incidence, as shown in Table 3-6. They represent 30.0 percent of the post-fisc

TABLE 3-6:   Social Goods

	Singles	Single Parents	One-Income Families	Two-Income Families	Seniors	Total
Poor						
Millions of dollars	2,834	2,142	2,571	1,656	3,268	12,472
Dollars per household	3,611	8,124	7,970	11,740	4,374	5,520
Percent of income	29.9%	33.2%	29.8%	38.9%	25.6%	30.0%
Low income						
Millions of dollars	1,736	1,243	2,618	3,233	2,863	11,693
Dollars per household	3,150	11,389	7,873	10,318	4,558	6,045
Percent of income	18.2%	31.7%	20.9%	25.5%	17.6%	21.3%
Lower-middle						
Millions of dollars	1,032	668	2,524	4,270	1,089	9,584
Dollars per household	2,809	8,150	6,843	8,790	4,601	6,220
Percent of income	13.1%	22.1%	15.6%	19.6%	11.9%	16.5%
Upper-middle						
Millions of dollars	1,384	395	2,628	7,545	971	12,924
Dollars per household	2,332	6,415	5,546	7,880	4,134	5,567
Percent of income	8.2%	13.4%	10.7%	14.4%	8.5%	11.9%
High income						
Millions of dollars	1,097	320	1,658	6,721	1,011	10,807
Dollars per household	2,335	13,031	5,456	6,405	4,908	5,263
Percent of income	5.2%	19.4%	7.6%	9.0%	6.7%	8.1%
Rich						
Millions of dollars	228	25	926	1,542	419	3,140
Dollars per household	4,754	17,455	10,572	9,564	9,060	9,117
Percent of income	4.8%	14.1%	6.4%	6.4%	6.7%	6.3%
All income classes						
Millions of dollars	8,312	4,793	12,926	24,968	9,621	60,620
Dollars per household	2,953	8,838	6,841	8,033	4,583	5,799
Percent of income	12.0%	26.4%	13.2%	13.2%	13.6%	13.6%

income of the poor and only 6.3 percent for the rich. In absolute amounts and per household these expenditures are similar for the first five income classes. However, on a per household basis the largest benefit accrues to the rich.

Among household types the largest expenditure for social goods accrues to two-income families, with 41.2 percent of the total, followed by one-income families (21.3 percent) and seniors (15.9 percent). One- and two-income families and seniors receive about the average benefit as a proportion of post-fisc income. Two family types stand out. Single-parent families receive a benefit of 26.4 percent of post-fisc income, almost double the average of 13.6 percent. Singles receive a benefit of 12 percent, which is below the average. On a per household basis, single-parent families and two-income families receive above-average benefits in every income class, while singles receive about 60 percent of the average in every class.

The two largest components of the social goods are health care and education. More details of the incidence of these expenditures are presented in Figure 3-2 for all households by 22 income classes.

As in the case of taxation, *one component dominates the redistributional impact of government purchases: health-care expenditures.* Figure 3-2 shows that, in 1986, *health-care benefits assigned to each income class as a percentage of its post-fisc income fell steadily from 20.1 percent for the bottom income class (below*

FIGURE 3-2:   Major Components of Government Purchases
             Ratio to Post-Fisc Income

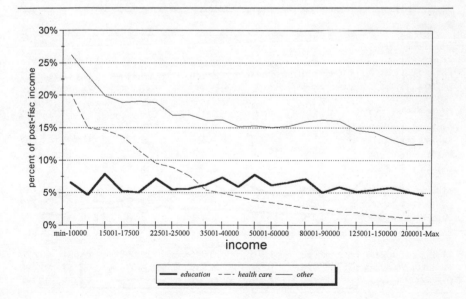

$10,000) to 1.2 percent for the income class above $200,000. Canadian households with income below $30,000 received an above-average share of health-care
expenditures (a share in excess of their share of post-fisc income), while those
with income above $30,000 received a below-average share. The pattern of these
effective benefits is highly progressive below $30,000 income and somewhat pro-
gressive thereafter.

Redistribution through the government provision of health care may also serve
other important economic and social objectives. It insulates the non-health spending
of low income households — which is mostly for necessities such as food, clothing and shelter — from non-discretionary fluctuations due to health conditions. It
stabilizes employment by reducing the health risks of those who could not afford
the payment of private costs. Finally, it reduces inequality of opportunity by eliminating the health advantage of those who can afford to pay for private health care.

Combined primary, secondary and postsecondary education generates very little redistribution by income class. For income groups below $80,000, the ratio to
post-fisc income fluctuated around the average value of 6.6 percent in 1986. Above
$80,000, there was a slight decline in that ratio. Considering the components of
education spending, shown in Figure 3-3, it can be seen that *the redistributional
impact of postsecondary education differs somewhat from that of primary and
secondary education, although not as much as is often thought.* Assuming that

FIGURE 3-3: Spending by Major Category
Education

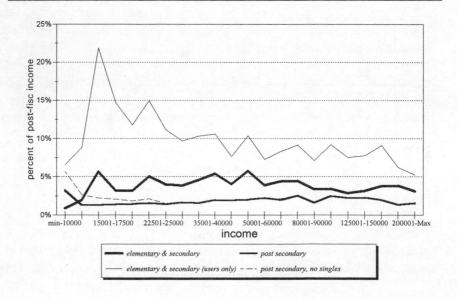

these expenditures benefit all households in proportion to the average number of school- and university-aged children (the dark lines), the benefit as a ratio to post-fisc income is relatively constant across income classes for both types of education. However, if we look at just the households with children in elementary or secondary school, the pattern of benefits is progressive above income of $15,000. The ratio of benefit to post-government income declines generally from 22 percent at $15,000 to 5 percent at incomes over $200,000. Removing the single student households from households with postsecondary students reduces the slight degree of progressivity at low incomes for postsecondary education.

While public education produces little direct redistribution, it may be argued that it generates substantial indirect redistribution. By providing opportunities for greater equality in educational attainment by children from different income classes, public education reduces potential inequality in earned income. This, in turn, lessens the need for income redistribution by government.

Government spending on goods and services that can be considered to be inter-mediate inputs into production, shown in Table 3-7, are slightly progressive. This category of expenditures is dominated by transportation which has a pattern of incidence similar, but in the opposite direction than motive fuel taxes. The benefit rate declines from 6.1 percent of post-fisc income for the poor to 3.5 percent for the rich. The largest share of expenditures (28.3 percent) is received by the high income class. On a per household basis, the rich receive $5,041, which is more than two and one-half times the average of $1,946. The middle class receives 37.2 percent of the total, more than its share of households. There is little difference in the benefits received among household types, except that singles receive about 40 percent more as a proportion of post-fisc income than other households.

The other purchases, in Table 3-8, account for only 1.5 percent of post-fisc income, but were by far the most progressively distributed of the four categories. They represent 8.1 percent of post-fisc income for the poor and only 0.3 percent for the rich. This results from the fact that the dominant expenditures in this group were purchases for social assistance and for labour, employment and immigration. For poor single parents and poor singles, these expenditures accounted for 19.1 percent and 13.6 percent of post-fisc income, respectively. These two groups accounted for 37.9 percent of the total expenditures.

Transfer Payments

TOTAL

Not surprisingly, transfer payments to persons generate redistribution in favour of low income groups. As shown in the previous chapter (Figure 2-3), the ratio of

TABLE 3-7: Intermediate Inputs

	Singles	Single Parents	One-Income Families	Two-Income Families	Seniors	Total
Poor						
Millions of dollars	911	285	409	212	705	2,521
Dollars per household	1,160	1,079	1,268	1,501	944	1,116
Percent of income	9.6%	4.4%	4.7%	5.0%	5.5%	6.1%
Low income						
Millions of dollars	723	157	538	603	733	2,755
Dollars per household	1,312	1,438	1,619	1,925	1,167	1,424
Percent of income	7.6%	4.0%	4.3%	4.8%	4.5%	5.0%
Lower-middle						
Millions of dollars	529	137	693	955	400	2,713
Dollars per household	1,439	1,667	1,878	1,965	1,689	1,760
Percent of income	6.7%	4.5%	4.3%	4.4%	4.4%	4.7%
Upper-middle						
Millions of dollars	993	133	1,077	2,199	454	4,856
Dollars per household	1,673	2,161	2,272	2,296	1,934	2,092
Percent of income	5.9%	4.5%	4.4%	4.2%	4.0%	4.5%
High income						
Millions of dollars	1,083	76	904	3,106	592	5,761
Dollars per household	2,305	3,105	2,974	2,960	2,872	2,805
Percent of income	5.2%	4.6%	4.2%	4.2%	3.9%	4.3%
Rich						
Millions of dollars	190	7	495	809	235	1,736
Dollars per household	3,964	4,960	5,653	5,016	5,083	5,041
Percent of income	4.0%	4.0%	3.4%	3.3%	3.8%	3.5%
All income classes						
Millions of dollars	4,429	795	4,116	7,884	3,119	20,342
Dollars per household	1,573	1,465	2,178	2,536	1,486	1,946
Percent of income	6.4%	4.4%	4.2%	4.2%	4.4%	4.6%

transfers to post-fisc income fell steadily in 1986 from 31.2 percent for the bottom income class to 0.8 percent for the top income class. The beneficiaries of this redistribution were those with income below $30,000, who received an above-average rate. This group received $29.9 billion in transfers, or 62.5 percent of the total. The rest ($17.9 billion, or 37.5 percent of the total) was received by those with income above $30,000.

TABLE 3-8: Other Purchases

	Singles	Single Parents	One-Income Families	Two-Income Families	Seniors	Total
Poor						
Millions of dollars	1,289	1,228	778	33	36	3,364
Dollars per household	1,642	4,657	2,411	237	49	1,489
Percent of income	13.6%	19.1%	9.0%	0.8%	0.3%	8.1%
Low income						
Millions of dollars	541	241	391	71	73	1,316
Dollars per household	982	2,209	1,175	225	116	681
Percent of income	5.7%	6.2%	3.1%	0.6%	0.4%	2.4%
Lower-middle						
Millions of dollars	215	84	254	58	53	664
Dollars per household	586	1,020	688	120	223	431
Percent of income	2.7%	2.8%	1.6%	0.3%	0.6%	1.1%
Upper-middle						
Millions of dollars	293	42	252	133	66	787
Dollars per household	494	681	532	139	283	339
Percent of income	1.7%	1.4%	1.0%	0.3%	0.6%	0.7%
High income						
Millions of dollars	167	17	130	187	53	554
Dollars per household	355	701	426	178	260	270
Percent of income	0.8%	1.0%	0.6%	0.3%	0.4%	0.4%
Rich						
Millions of dollars	28	1	30	52	15	126
Dollars per household	580	1,027	345	322	322	367
Percent of income	0.6%	0.8%	0.2%	0.2%	0.2%	0.3%
All income classes						
Millions of dollars	2,533	1,613	1,834	535	297	6,812
Dollars per household	900	2,975	971	172	141	652
Percent of income	3.7%	8.9%	1.9%	0.3%	0.4%	1.5%

The pattern of the ratio of transfers to post-fisc income is more progressive than the personal income tax for income classes below $30,000, but tapers off very gradually at higher incomes. The redistributive effect is lower than the PIT, however, because of the smaller amount of money redistributed. The class below $10,000 is made 18.5 percent better off than under a proportional distribution of transfers and the class above $200,000 is made 9 percent worse off. This progressive redistributional impact is largely caused by the income testing of some major transfers, such as social assistance, the Guaranteed Income Supplement (GIS), Old Age Security (OAS), provincial senior top-ups, and the child tax credit.

In our view, *the major issue with respect to transfer payments is not how much redistribution they generate, but why a large portion of transfers is provided to those with above-average income.* Transfers represent a significant net addition to post-fisc income only for those households with income below $20,000. The relative economic position of households with income between $20,000 and $45,000 is not significantly affected by transfers, while those above $45,000 are net losers. In order to shed some light on this issue, we provide detailed information on the distribution of transfer payments by household type and major income class in Table 3-9.

For all income classes, total transfer payments amounted to $47.9 billion or nearly $4,600 per household in 1986. They represented 10.7 percent of post-fisc income. This total includes $3.3 million of pensions received by public employees. We exclude these from our discussion in this section, and from Table 3-9, as they do not represent deliberate instruments of redistribution and pensions received by retired private sector employees are not included as transfers. Moreover, since nearly 60 percent of those pensions are received by seniors, their inclusion would lead to misleading comparisons between seniors and non-seniors. The adjusted total transfers amounted to $44.6 billion and represented $4,267 per household and 10.0 percent of post-fisc income.

Of this adjusted total amount, 39.8 percent was received by senior households, 19.7 percent by one-income, two-parent households and 19.3 percent by two-income households. Single and single-parent households received 14.4 percent and 6.8 percent, respectively. *On a per household basis, seniors are the biggest beneficiaries of transfers to persons. At $8,462, the amount of transfers they received is nearly double the average.* The next two largest beneficiaries are single parents and one-income households, with benefits 31 percent and 9 percent above average, respectively.

Slightly more than one-quarter of transfer payments (26.5 percent) was received by the poor. Their benefit per household was 22.6 percent above the average. Almost an equal amount (and a higher amount per household) was received by the low income class. One-third of transfers was received by the middle income class, almost equal to its share of households. Transfers to the upper-middle class equalled over two-thirds of the transfers to the poor. The high income class and the rich, combined, received more than half of the amount of total transfers and transfers per household received by the poor.

Since about 40 percent of transfers were received by seniors, it is not surprising to note that the distribution of transfers by income class is significantly affected

TABLE 3-9:   Transfers Received by Family Type
             Government Pension Set to Zero

	Single	Total SPF	Total 1 Income	Total 2 Income	Total Seniors	Combined Total
Poor						
Millions of dollars	2,059	1,743	2,095	479	5,444	11,820
Dollars per household	2,623	6,611	6,495	3,394	7,286	5,231
Percent of income	21.7%	27.0%	24.2%	11.3%	42.6%	28.4%
Low income						
Millions of dollars	1,657	655	1,964	1,364	5,445	11,085
Dollars per household	3,006	6,007	5,905	4,353	8,668	5,730
Percent of income	17.3%	16.7%	15.7%	10.8%	33.5%	20.2%
Lower-middle						
Millions of dollars	928	341	1,649	1,716	2,318	6,952
Dollars per household	2,523	4,156	4,470	3,533	9,797	4,512
Percent of income	11.8%	11.3%	10.2%	7.9%	25.3%	12.0%
Upper-middle						
Millions of dollars	1,058	229	1,818	2,621	2,286	8,012
Dollars per household	1,782	3,717	3,836	2,737	9,732	3,451
Percent of income	6.3%	7.7%	7.4%	5.0%	19.9%	7.4%
High income						
Millions of dollars	660	69	1,050	2,157	1,844	5,780
Dollars per household	1,405	2,801	3,454	2,056	8,950	2,814
Percent of income	3.2%	4.2%	4.8%	2.9%	12.3%	4.3%
Rich						
Millions of dollars	79	6	192	260	426	962
Dollars per household	1,648	3,910	2,189	1,609	9,209	2,792
Percent of income	1.7%	3.2%	1.3%	1.1%	6.8%	1.9%
All income classes						
Millions of dollars	6,440	3,042	8,768	8,597	17,763	44,610
Dollars per household	2,288	5,610	4,640	2,766	8,462	4,267
Percent of income	9.3%	16.7%	8.9%	4.5%	25.0%	10.0%

by the distribution of transfers to seniors. *Among households headed by seniors, 25.6 percent of transfers were received by the top half of the income distribution. This amount was equal to 83.7 percent of the transfers received by poor seniors.* The middle class received 25.9 percent of transfers to seniors, equivalent to 84.6 percent of the amount received by the poor. *On a per household basis, the poor was the only income class among seniors that received below-average transfers,* primarily because it includes largely single seniors. Seniors in all income classes received above-average transfers per household. *Rich seniors received, per household, more than double the average per household transfers of the whole population and 76 percent more than the average per capita transfers of the poor.*

Transfers accessed by non-seniors also provided substantial benefits to the middle class and to the top two income classes. The former received 38.6 percent and the latter 16.7 percent of total transfers to non-seniors. A particularly interesting result is that 58.6 percent of the transfers received by two-income families went to those with above the median income. On a per household basis, poor single and poor two-income households received below the average transfers of all households.

The redistributional impact of transfers is more appropriately analyzed using the pattern of the ratio of transfers to post-fisc income, also shown in Table 3-9. As shown for a more detailed income distribution in Figure 2-3, a progressive pattern of effective benefit rates is clearly visible. Their 1986 values fell from 28.4 percent to 1.9 percent from the bottom to the top major income class. The fall in the effective benefit rate is largest in the case of seniors; the 35.8 percentage point difference is one-third higher than the average reduction of 26.5 percentage points. Single-parent, one-income and single households also have a very progressive pattern of benefits, with the effective rates declining by 23.8, 22.9 and 20 percentage points, respectively. Two-income families experience a reduction of only 10.2 percentage points.

The main conclusion we derive from the above discussion is that the Canadian transfer system as a whole is not designed primarily to perform a Robin Hood function. When Canadians in the top half of the income distribution receive over a quarter of all government transfer payments, it is hard to conclude that those transfers have been effectively targeted for redistribution.

NET REDISTRIBUTIONAL IMPACT OF TRANSFERS

An alternative view of the redistributional impact of transfers is provided by considering the benefits net of the associated tax financing. In calculating the net benefit of the transfer-tax package, we assumed that total transfers to persons, excluding public service pensions, were financed first by dedicated tax sources, including UI premiums, WCB premiums and CPP/QPP contributions. The remaining revenue short-fall was assumed to be financed by the average tax mix of the federal and provincial governments. We excluded municipalities because they spend very little on transfers. This removes the property tax from the financing base.

It must be stressed that is a hypothetical exercise involving some strong assumptions, therefore, the results are not directly comparable to those for the actual fiscal incidence. First, it needs to be recognized in this exercise that a large share of transfers is related to the social insurance function and that those programs

— UI, CPP/QPP and WCB — are financed through dedicated payroll taxes, though there is not a perfect match between benefits and payments because of the lack of full funding. Second, it is assumed that social assistance type of programs are fully financed through taxation using the existing tax mix. The results, therefore, should be interpreted as what the net redistributional impact of transfers would be *if* the above assumptions held.

Table 3-10 provides estimates of net transfer benefits by household type and major income class for 1986. Not surprisingly, the net transfer benefits are more progressively (pro-poor) distributed than the gross benefits because taxes reinforce the progressive pattern of transfers.

Of total net transfers of $24 billion, almost 45 percent ($10.6 billion) was received by the poor; an additional 32.9 percent was received by the low income class. The largest contribution was made by the high income class with a net loss of $10.1 billion. On a per household basis, the low income class received almost as much ($4,078) as the poor ($4,682). These net amounts represent a quarter of post-fisc income for the poor and 14.4 percent for the low income class.

On a net basis, the biggest winner from transfers among household types is seniors; in 1986 senior households received $16.6 billion in transfers net of tax. Seniors in the first five income classes benefited substantially from net transfers. Rich seniors incurred a small loss. The largest per household benefit ($9,635) was received by lower-middle income seniors, followed by low income seniors ($9,032) and upper-middle income seniors ($8,768). High income seniors received per household net transfers equal to 76 percent of those received by poor seniors and 19.5 percent greater than transfers to the poor as a whole (including poor seniors). Net transfers comprised 23.3 percent of the post-fisc income of seniors on average, declining from 43.0 percent for the poor to 7.7 percent for the high income class and -1.5 percent for the rich.

The main contributor to net transfers among household types was two-income families, who paid $14.4 billion in taxes net of transfers received. Combined upper-middle and high income, two-income households paid nearly 80 percent of this amount ($11.4 billion). Among the other household types, single-parent families gained $1.7 billion, while singles and one-income families were net contributors of $2.8 billion and $1.2 billion, respectively.

Major Transfers to Persons

In the following sections we analyze the major components of the transfer payment package. Because seniors as a group are the largest beneficiaries of government transfers, we will start with a review of the programs that benefit them.

TABLE 3-10:   Redistributional Impact of Transfer Payments
             Combined Benefits and Financing

	Singles	Single Parents	One-Income Families	Two-Income Families	Seniors	Total
Poor						
Millions of dollars	1,444	1,586	1,827	225	5,497	10,579
Dollars per household	1,840	6,015	5,662	1,593	7,358	4,682
Percent of income	15.2%	24.6%	21.1%	5.3%	43.0%	25.4%
Low income						
Millions of dollars	752	387	904	171	5,674	7,888
Dollars per household	1,364	3,550	2,717	547	9,032	4,078
Percent of income	7.9%	9.9%	7.2%	1.4%	34.9%	14.4%
Lower-middle						
Millions of dollars	(211)	(1)	(157)	(925)	2,280	986
Dollars per household	(573)	(14)	(426)	(1,903)	9,635	640
Percent of income	-2.7%	-0.0%	-1.0%	-4.2%	24.9%	1.7%
Upper-middle						
Millions of dollars	(1,763)	(122)	(1,118)	(4,126)	2,060	(5,069)
Dollars per household	(2,970)	(1,982)	(2,358)	(4,309)	8,768	(2,183)
Percent of income	-10.5%	-4.1%	-4.6%	-7.9%	17.9%	-4.7%
High income						
Millions of dollars	(2,530)	(123)	(1,360)	(7,255)	1,152	(10,116)
Dollars per household	(5,385)	(5,010)	(4,475)	(6,915)	5,594	(4,926)
Percent of income	-12.1%	-7.5%	-6.3%	-9.8%	7.7%	-7.6%
Rich						
Millions of dollars	(458)	(18)	(1,248)	(2,448)	(96)	(4,268)
Dollars per household	(9,557)	(12,614)	(14,257)	(15,181)	(2,066)	(12,392)
Percent of income	-9.7%	-10.2%	-8.6%	-10.1%	-1.5%	-8.6%
All income classes						
Millions of dollars	(2,765)	1,709	(1,153)	(14,358)	16,568	(0)
Dollars per household	(982)	3,152	(610)	(4,619)	7,893	(0)
Percent of income	-4.0%	9.4%	-1.2%	-7.6%	23.3%	-0.0%

TRANSFERS TO SENIORS

The fiscal system contains a variety of measures specifically directed at assisting
seniors. Some of those measures are provided through the tax system; others are
delivered directly as transfer payments. Since income assistance delivered through
the personal income tax is incorporated in the redistributional impact of the tax
system, we will confine our discussion to direct transfer payments.

Nearly 88 percent of the transfers received by seniors in 1986 originated from three major programs: Old Age Security (OAS) (43.2 percent), the Canada and Quebec Pension Plan (CPP/QPP) (26.2 percent) and the federal Guaranteed Income Supplement plus provincial supplements (GIS&S) (18.5 percent). The remaining 12 percent (called other) includes a variety of transfers, such as Veterans' benefits and Workers' Compensation benefits.

The effective benefit rates on post-fisc income for each of the above four major components of transfers to seniors in 1986 are shown in Figure 3-4. All four components are generally progressive (pro-poor) overall, as the effective benefit rates fall when income increases. *The GIS&S is by far the most progressive component, as a result of being income-tested.* Its effective rate drops from 17.4 to 1.5 percent at an income of $25,000 and then slowly moves to zero.

The next most progressive item is OAS because it is a universal demogrant of fixed amount. Its effective rate starts at the same level as GIS&S, but falls at a slower pace, reaching 0.9 percent at the top income class. In 1989 the OAS was income-tested through a personal income tax claw-back at a rate of 15 percent of individual net income (for income tax) exceeding $50,000 (indexed to the Consumer Price Index less 3 percent). As a result of this change, the benefits of OAS are distributed in a slightly more progressive manner over higher classes than in 1986.

CPP/QPP is progressive overall, but because it is based on contributions out of earned income during the working years, benefits per senior household increase

FIGURE 3-4:   Transfers to Seniors

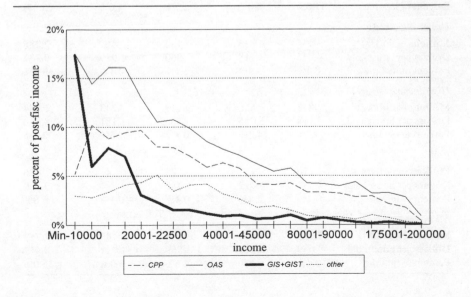

with income until the maximum is reached. The effective benefit ratio to post-fisc income rises from 5 percent to 10 percent at about $12,000 in 1986 and declines very gradually above $20,000 to 0.4 percent for seniors over $200,000.

All other transfers, as a group, have a slightly inverted U pattern of benefit rates skewed to the right. The combined benefit rate increases up to income of $22,000 and then declines gradually, reaching 0.2 percent for the top income class.

Table 3-11 provides additional information by broad income class on the cash amounts of transfers to seniors, total and per household, for the above four major

TABLE 3-11:   Selected Transfers to Seniors

	OAS	C/QPP	GIS/S	Other	Total Transfers
Poor					
Millions of dollars	2,281	761	2,005	397	5,444
Dollars per household	3,054	1,018	2,683	531	7,286
Percent of income	17.9%	6.0%	15.7%	3.1%	42.6%
Low income					
Millions of dollars	2,381	1,631	863	570	5,445
Dollars per household	3,791	2,596	1,374	907	8,668
Percent of income	14.6%	10.0%	5.3%	3.5%	33.5%
Lower-middle					
Millions of dollars	1,005	732	156	425	2,318
Dollars per household	4,248	3,093	659	1,798	9,797
Percent of income	11.0%	8.0%	1.7%	4.6%	25.3%
Upper-middle					
Millions of dollars	955	733	132	467	2,286
Dollars per household	4,065	3,118	560	1,989	9,732
Percent of income	8.3%	6.4%	1.1%	4.1%	19.9%
High income					
Millions of dollars	848	636	117	243	1,844
Dollars per household	4,118	3,085	566	1,181	8,950
Percent of income	5.7%	4.2%	0.8%	1.6%	12.3%
Rich					
Millions of dollars	210	153	22	41	426
Dollars per household	4,537	3,312	480	881	9,209
Percent of income	3.4%	2.4%	0.4%	0.7%	6.8%
All income classes					
Millions of dollars	7,681	4,645	3,294	2,143	17,763
Dollars per household	3,659	2,213	1,569	1,021	8,462
Percent of income	10.8%	6.5%	4.6%	3.0%	25.0%

components. *In the case of OAS, nearly 30 percent was received by the poor. The middle class received 25.5 percent and the top two income classes combined received 13.8 percent. On a per household basis, rich seniors received the largest OAS benefit and poor seniors the least.*[6] The income-testing of OAS, introduced in 1989, has eliminated some of the benefits to the top income class, but has left unchanged the benefits to the middle class, broadly defined.

The largest share of benefits from the CPP/QPP was received by the low income class, with over one-third of the total. The poor, the lower middle class and the upper middle class received nearly equal shares (about 16 percent each). On a per household basis the biggest beneficiary was the rich, with a benefit ($3,312) 50 percent higher than the average. Benefits of nearly $3,100 per household were received by the lower-middle, upper-middle and high income class. The benefit per household received by the poor was less than one-half the average.

The shares of benefits from the income-tested GIS and provincial top-ups further reveals that this is the only strongly progressive major transfer to seniors. Over 60 percent of the total expenditure went to poor seniors. An additional 26.2 percent went to the low income class. On a per household basis the poor received 71 percent above the average benefit and all other income classes received below the average benefit.

In conclusion, a large share of transfers to seniors is received by those in the middle and upper income classes. In the case of CPP/QPP, this result may serve a policy objective, since the benefits are similar to those for a private pension and, therefore, are related to contributions made. In the case of OAS, the results are less clearly related to the policy objectives.

UNEMPLOYMENT INSURANCE

Among the transfer payments not specifically targeted to seniors, Unemployment Insurance benefits are by far the largest, accounting for 19.2 percent of total net transfers to persons in 1986. As shown in Figure 3-5, *UI benefits as a ratio to post-fisc income exhibit an inverted U pattern skewed to the right.* Since benefits are a percentage of wages received during the qualifying period, up to a maximum, the benefit rate increases up to income of $17,500 and then falls steadily as income increases.

Table 3-12 shows that the bulk of UI benefits were received by one-income households (30.8 percent) and two-income households (39.7 percent). Singles also received a fairly large share of benefits (21.3 percent). Relatively small amounts were received by single-parent households (4.8 percent) and households headed by a senior (3.3 percent). The one-income and two-income households were the only groups who received above-average benefits per household. However, the benefit to post-fisc income ratio tells another side of the story. The largest

FIGURE 3-5:   Transfers to Non-Seniors
                    SA, UI and Other

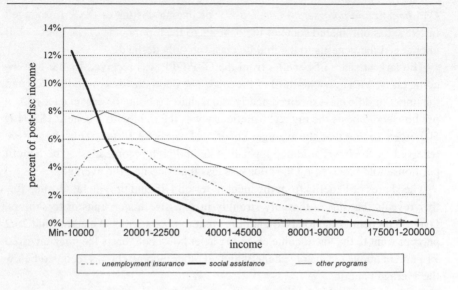

benefit ratio was received by one-income households (2.7 percent), followed closely by singles (2.6 percent) and single-parent households (2.3 percent). Two-income households received about the average benefit rate (1.9 percent), while seniors received a benefit rate (0.4 percent) well below the average.

Table 3-12 also shows that the poor income class received only 12.7 percent of total UI benefits, less than the benefits received by the high income class (17.8 percent). Almost 25 percent of total benefits went to the upper-middle income class. The low and lower-middle income classes received the largest benefits per household, with amounts 22.2 percent and 39.7 percent above the average, respectively. The poor received per household benefits equal to just 60 percent of the average, less than the benefit to the rich.

It may be argued that in order to make general statements about the redistributional impact of the UI program we must look at both the benefit and cost side of the program. This comparison is facilitated by the fact that the UI benefits are financed by a dedicated tax source, employer and employee payroll contributions.

Estimates of the net UI benefits by selected household types and major income classes are shown in Table 3-13. Our calculation assumes that both employer and employee contributions are ultimately borne by wage earners.

TABLE 3-12:   Gross Unemployment Insurance Benefits

	Singles	Single Parents	One-Income Families	Two-Income Families	Seniors	Total
Poor						
Millions of dollars	313	128	510	137	4	1,093
Dollars per household	399	486	1,580	971	6	484
Percent of income	3.3%	2.0%	5.9%	3.2%	0.0%	2.6%
Low income						
Millions of dollars	615	151	588	546	40	1,939
Dollars per household	1,116	1,381	1,768	1,742	63	1,003
Percent of income	6.4%	3.8%	4.7%	4.3%	0.2%	3.5%
Lower-middle						
Millions of dollars	370	93	487	740	78	1,768
Dollars per household	1,008	1,131	1,319	1,523	330	1,147
Percent of income	4.7%	3.1%	3.0%	3.4%	0.9%	3.0%
Upper-middle						
Millions of dollars	316	39	602	1,031	94	2,082
Dollars per household	533	631	1,270	1,077	399	897
Percent of income	1.9%	1.3%	2.5%	2.0%	0.8%	1.9%
High income						
Millions of dollars	187	12	395	874	59	1,527
Dollars per household	398	500	1,299	833	287	744
Percent of income	0.9%	0.7%	1.8%	1.2%	0.4%	1.1%
Rich						
Millions of dollars	22	1	62	85	5	175
Dollars per household	459	459	710	529	114	509
Percent of income	0.5%	0.4%	0.4%	0.4%	0.1%	0.4%
All income classes						
Millions of dollars	1,825	423	2,643	3,412	280	8,584
Dollars per household	648	780	1,399	1,098	134	821
Percent of income	2.6%	2.3%	2.7%	1.8%	0.4%	1.9%

For all households, the net UI benefits have a mildly progressive (pro-poor) pattern of incidence: the poor income class received $1.1 billion of net benefits, somewhat less than the amount paid by the top two income classes. The largest net beneficiary was the low income class ($1.4 billion), with 45.7 percent of total net benefits. The middle class essentially ended up even, with the upper middle class transferring over $0.5 billion to the lower middle class. On a per household basis, the net gain is highest for the low income class and the net gain of the lower middle class is 70.5 percent of that of the poor.

TABLE 3-13:   Net Unemployment Insurance Benefits
Gross Unemployment Insurance Less Premiums

	Singles	Single Parents	One-Income Families	Two-Income Families	Seniors	Total
Poor						
Millions of dollars	295	130	551	107	4	1,086
Dollars per household	376	493	1,707	758	5	481
Percent of income	3.1%	2.0%	6.4%	2.5%	0.0%	2.6%
Low income						
Millions of dollars	515	106	400	332	35	1,388
Dollars per household	934	973	1,204	1,061	55	718
Percent of income	5.4%	2.7%	3.2%	2.6%	0.2%	2.5%
Lower-middle						
Millions of dollars	145	16	100	197	65	522
Dollars per household	394	198	272	405	274	339
Percent of income	1.8%	0.5%	0.6%	0.9%	0.7%	0.9%
Upper-middle						
Millions of dollars	(378)	(43)	9	(252)	32	(633)
Dollars per household	(637)	(707)	18	(263)	134	(273)
Percent of income	-2.3%	-1.5%	0.0%	-0.5%	0.3%	-0.6%
High income						
Millions of dollars	(503)	(23)	(9)	(602)	(116)	(1,253)
Dollars per household	(1,072)	(931)	(30)	(574)	(563)	(610)
Percent of income	-2.4%	-1.4%	-0.0%	-0.8%	-0.8%	-0.9%
Rich						
Millions of dollars	(49)	(1)	(65)	(152)	(64)	(331)
Dollars per household	(1,015)	(903)	(741)	(945)	(1,386)	(962)
Percent of income	-1.0%	-0.7%	-0.4%	-1.1%	-1.0%	-0.7%
All income classes						
Millions of dollars	24	185	986	(370)	(46)	779
Dollars per household	9	341	522	(119)	(22)	75
Percent of income	0.0%	1.0%	1.0%	-0.2%	-0.1%	0.2%

Among household types, the big gainers ($986 million) are one-income fami-
lies followed by single-parent families ($185 million). Singles end up almost even,
while two-income families and seniors are net losers with losses of $370 million
and $46 million, respectively. On a per household basis, the net gain is higher for
one-income families ($522) than for single-parent families ($341); this was 1 percent of post-fisc income for both household types.

SOCIAL ASSISTANCE

Social assistance is strictly targeted to households with at least temporarily low income; therefore, one would expect the benefit rates to have a very progressive (pro-poor) pattern. As shown in Figure 3-5, *effective benefit rates for social assistance drop sharply to income of $20,000 and then fall more slowly, but reach a value of less than 1 percent at an income of $40,000.* Social assistance payments make up 12 percent of post-fisc income for the lowest income class.

Despite this progressive pattern of benefit rates, a considerable share (15.2 percent) of social assistance benefits is received by households with above-median income. As shown in Table 3-14, *nearly 45 percent of social assistance benefits in 1986 were received by households not considered to be poor.* The middle class received nearly as much in benefits (19.1 percent) as the low income class (20.1 percent). On a per household basis, by far the largest benefit ($1,256) is received by the poor, more than twice the average value of $490. The low income class also received per household benefits ($532) above the average.

Among household types, the largest share of benefits was received by singles (40.4 percent), followed by one-income families (28.0 percent) and single-parent families (26.7 percent). *By far the largest per household benefit was received by single-parent families, at over five times the average.* One-income families and singles also received above average per household benefits. Social assistance benefits accounted for 7.5 percent of the post-fisc income of single parents, and 3.0 percent and 1.5 percent of singles and one-income families, respectively.

OTHER TRANSFERS TO NON-SENIORS

This category includes a variety of transfers such as Workers' Compensation Board benefits, transfers to charities, education grants and scholarships and financial assistance to natives. As shown in Figure 3-5, they also exhibit a progressive pattern of effective benefit rates, but not as progressive as social assistance. The benefit rate, which is approximately 8 percent at the bottom end of the income scale, is still about 4 percent at income of $40,000 and 2 percent at income of $80,000.

Table 3-15 shows that the poor income class received 24.6 percent of other transfers, just 64.7 percent of the amount received by the middle income classes, in 1986. The high income class received 13.7 percent of the total benefits, 55.8 percent of that received by the poor. On a per household basis, income classes below the median received above-average benefits. However, the rich received per household over one half of the benefit received by the poor.

As in the case of unemployment benefits, the bulk of other transfers are received by two-income families (30.8 percent) and one-income families (29.3 percent).

TABLE 3-14:   Selected Transfers by Major Family Category
              Social Assistance Benefits

	Singles	Single Parents	One-Income Families	Two-Income Families	Seniors	Total
Poor						
Millions of dollars	1,098	1,053	660	25	1	2,837
Dollars per household	1,399	3,992	2,047	177	1	1,256
Percent of income	11.6%	16.3%	7.6	0.6%	0.0%	6.8%
Low income						
Millions of dollars	451	203	320	46	9	1,029
Dollars per household	819	1,862	962	147	14	532
Percent of income	4.7%	5.2%	2.6%	0.4%	0.1%	1.9%
Lower-middle						
Millions of dollars	172	68	196	22	19	476
Dollars per household	468	830	530	44	81	309
Percent of income	2.2%	2.3%	1.2%	0.1%	0.2%	0.8%
Upper-middle						
Millions of dollars	224	31	179	39	27	500
Dollars per household	377	511	377	41	116	215
Percent of income	1.3%	1.1%	0.7%	0.1%	0.2%	0.5%
High income						
Millions of dollars	107	12	77	46	12	254
Dollars per household	229	505	252	43	60	124
Percent of income	0.5%	0.8%	0.4%	0.1%	0.1%	0.2%
Rich						
Millions of dollars	16	1	2	5	0	24
Dollars per household	331	649	26	30	0	69
Percent of income	0.3%	0.5%	0.0%	0.0%	0.0%	0.0%
All income classes						
Millions of dollars	2,068	1,368	1,433	182	68	5,120
Dollars per household	735	2,523	759	58	33	490
Percent of income	3.0%	7.5%	1.5%	0.1%	0.1%	1.1%

Singles receive 20.9 percent, while single-parent and senior households shared 19.1 percent almost equally. On a per household basis, single-parent and one-income families received above-average benefits. As a share of post-fisc income, the largest beneficiaries were single-parent families (16.1 percent) followed by one-income families and singles (8.2 percent).

TABLE 3-15: Other Non-Senior Transfers
(All Transfers Excluding CPP/QPP, OAS, GIS/S, Veterans
Pension, Pensions to Government Employees)

	Singles	Single Parents	One-Income Families	Two-Income Families	Seniors	Total
Poor						
Millions of dollars	1,921	1,717	2,001	473	622	6,734
Dollars per household	2,448	6,512	6,202	3,351	832	2,980
Percent of income	20.2%	26.6%	23.2%	11.1%	4.9%	16.2%
Low income						
Millions of dollars	1,505	619	1,841	1,353	649	5,968
Dollars per household	2,731	5,676	5,537	4,319	1,033	3,085
Percent of income	15.8%	15.8%	14.7%	10.7%	4.0%	10.9%
Lower-middle						
Millions of dollars	806	323	1,544	1,699	373	4,745
Dollars per household	2,194	3,937	4,187	3,496	1,577	3,080
Percent of income	10.3%	10.7%	9.5%	7.8%	4.1%	8.2%
Upper-middle						
Millions of dollars	907	198	1,613	2,562	378	5,657
Dollars per household	1,528	3,216	3,403	2,675	1,609	2,437
Percent of income	5.4%	6.7%	6.6%	4.9%	3.3%	5.2%
High income						
Millions of dollars	511	59	864	2,081	242	3,758
Dollars per household	1,087	2,414	2,844	1,984	1,177	1,830
Percent of income	2.4%	3.6%	4.0%	2.8%	1.6%	2.8%
Rich						
Millions of dollars	62	4	156	253	45	520
Dollars per household	1,293	2,639	1,783	1,571	966	1,509
Percent of income	1.3%	2.1%	1.1%	1.0%	0.7%	1.0%
All income classes						
Millions of dollars	5,713	2,920	8,020	8,421	2,309	27,383
Dollars per household	2,029	5,385	4,245	2,709	1,100	2,619
Percent of income	8.2%	16.1%	8.2%	4.4%	3.3%	6.1%

Transfers to Business

So far we have discussed transfers to persons. Governments, however, also provide transfers to businesses in the form of direct and indirect subsidies. These are effectively indirect transfers to persons, as they ultimately benefit consumers or the recipients of factor income (wages and profits). We included transfers to business in total government purchases for our fiscal incidence calculations because they do not involve a direct transfer to persons. However, we evaluate them in this section to draw attention to their nature as transfers. *Transfers to business amounted to $14.1 billion in 1986, representing 3.2 percent of post-fisc income, or $1,351 per household. Agricultural subsidies represented 28.5 percent of this total.*

Although these transfers are usually motivated by reasons other than vertical redistribution, on the whole they deliver a mild degree of redistribution in favour of lower income groups. As shown in Figure 3-6, the ratio of these transfers to post-fisc income fluctuated around a slight downward trend to income of about $90,000 and fell rapidly thereafter. This mild progressivity is due largely to transfers other than agricultural subsidies, which exhibit a steadily declining pattern of effective benefit rates.

Agricultural subsidies, on the other hand, show an erratic but overall regressive pattern of effective benefit rates. These rates first increase sharply to income of $22,500, are largely constant, with fluctuations, to income of about $80,000, edge up to their maximum value at income of $90,000 and then fall steadily. Both the bottom and top income groups received a below-average benefit rate. This pattern reflects the distribution of agricultural income, since the subsidies were

FIGURE 3-6:   Transfers to Business

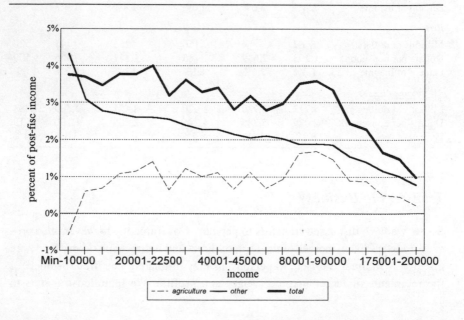

allocated to net farm income on the assumption that agricultural products are tradeable goods in a small open economy.

More details on the redistributional impact of business subsidies are found in Table 3-16. Of the total subsidies of $14.1 billion in 1986, 38 percent was received by the middle income classes (primarily the upper-middle class with a share of 23.9 percent). The poor received only 11.2 percent of the subsidies, just over one-third of the share received by the high income class (29.7 percent). The latter was the largest beneficiary with benefits of $4.2 billion. Over 60 percent of

TABLE 3-16: All Transfers to Business

	Singles	Single Parents	One-Income Families	Two-Income Families	Seniors	Total
Poor						
Millions of dollars	546	167	305	211	347	1,576
Dollars per household	696	634	946	1,495	465	698
Percent of income	5.8%	2.6%	3.5%	5.0%	2.7%	3.8%
Low income						
Millions of dollars	474	91	363	650	396	1,975
Dollars per household	860	835	1,093	2,075	631	1,021
Percent of income	5.0%	2.3%	2.9%	5.1%	2.4%	3.6%
Lower-middle						
Millions of dollars	341	76	488	836	250	1,992
Dollars per household	928	925	1,324	1,722	1,057	1,293
Percent of income	4.3%	2.5%	3.0%	3.8%	2.7%	3.4%
Upper-middle						
Millions of dollars	617	73	777	1,629	276	3,373
Dollars per household	1,040	1,185	1,641	1,701	1,176	1,453
Percent of income	3.7%	2.5%	3.2%	3.1%	2.4%	3.1%
High income						
Millions of dollars	715	48	651	2,362	420	4,196
Dollars per household	1,523	1,939	2,141	2,251	2,040	2,043
Percent of income	3.4%	2.9%	3.0%	3.2%	2.8%	3.1%
Rich						
Millions of dollars	107	3	264	497	136	1,008
Dollars per household	2,227	2,147	3,015	3,084	2,949	2,925
Percent of income	2.3%	1.7%	1.8%	2.1%	2.2%	2.0%
All income classes						
Millions of dollars	2,800	458	2,849	6,185	1,827	14,119
Dollars per household	995	844	1,508	1,990	870	1,351
Percent of income	4.0%	2.5%	2.9%	3.3%	2.6%	3.2%

total business subsidies went to households above the median income. *On a per household basis, the largest benefit went to the rich income class, with over twice the average and over four times that received by the poor, which received the least.*

Nearly 44 percent of the subsidies benefited two-income families, and an additional 40 percent benefited one-income families and singles almost equally. On a per household basis, only one- and two-income families received above-average benefits (11.6 percent and 47.3 percent above the average, respectively). The highest effective benefit rate was received by singles (4.0 percent) and the lowest by seniors (2.6 percent) and single parents (2.5 percent).

Concluding Comment on Transfers

When we consider all government transfer payments, including subsidies to business, one aspect is striking: the amount of transfers going to households considered to be neither poor nor low income. If pensions to civil servants are excluded, non-poor households received nearly three-quarters of gross transfers and households classified as middle class or above received nearly half of gross transfers. The latter's share of transfers (48.7 percent) is not much lower than its share of households (59.8 percent).

In 1986, an estimated 16¢ per dollar of taxes paid by households with middle and higher income was returned to them in the form of transfer payments. For the middle income class this value was 25¢. A substantial portion of the taxes paid by the middle income class serves a largely insurance function, from which they benefit directly.

The poor received a net redistribution from transfers of $11.8 billion, equivalent to just over 25 cents per dollar of gross transfers. It seems that the Canadian transfers to persons system in 1986 was equally directed at the redistribution and social insurance functions of government.

NOTES

1. For the very small group of rich single-parent families, the measured PIT burden is much higher than in all other family-income groups. As mentioned earlier, this result is unreliable.
2. Senior households have a small average number of dependents, while singles, by definition, have none. Senior couples, however, are effectively two-income households, since both receive at least the basic level of government transfer income.

3. Statistics Canada's *Family Expenditure in Canada, 1986*, (Table 16) reports that 78 percent of senior married couple families owned their own homes, against 75 percent of all married couple families. For unattached individuals, about 40 percent of seniors own their homes, against 30 percent overall. Senior married couples spent 13.5 percent of their food expenditure on restaurant meals, while the rate for all married couples was 23.5 percent. Only 33.5 percent of senior married couples reported expenditures on furniture, while the overall rate was 55 percent, and the average expenditure of senior couples was about 45 percent of that of all married couples. Appliance expenditures were similar. Package travel tours were purchased by 12 percent of senior married couples with no dependent (others were not reported), against 10.5 percent for all married couples without dependents, while the average expenditure of the senior family was 70 percent greater than the overall average.

4. Flat taxes for Canada were analyzed by R. Smith (1986).

5. In Chapter 2, transfers to business were included in government purchases. These are discussed below in the section on transfer payments.

6. On a per household basis, the poor received below-average benefits, largely because they contain an above-average proportion of single seniors. OAS is not adjusted for family size, so senior couples receive double that of singles. However, the income equivalency used to adjust for family size in the definition of the six broad income classes is 0.4.

CHAPTER FOUR

Equity and Redistribution

The previous two chapters presented some estimates of the degree of redistribution in Canada for the year 1986. The results almost automatically raise the question: Did the Canadian fiscal system generate too much or too little redistribution in 1986? There may be no objective answer to this question, since different people hold different principles about the definition of equity and the role of government in income redistribution.[1]

An important distinction in the definition of equity is that between process and outcome. If the processes underlying employment, education and earnings do not involve discriminatory practices or the exercise of market power, one may say that there is equity in the economic system. In this case, equity can be interpreted as the provision of equality of opportunity.

Even an equitable process does not guarantee a distribution of income that is considered equitable by society. The pursuit of equity in this case involves deliberate decisions to alter market outcomes. Maintaining equality of opportunities under a market economy may be viewed partly as an objective exercise, but correcting inequalities of outcomes necessarily involves value judgements expressed through the political process.

Equity has both vertical and horizontal dimensions even within the framework of annual income redistribution. Applied to taxation, horizontal equity means that individuals or families in similar economic circumstances should pay similar amounts of taxes. Vertical equity in taxation basically means that the rich should pay tax at higher rates than the poor. By the same reasoning, the rich would receive proportionally less benefits from government expenditures than the poor. Applied to income redistribution, the concept of vertical equity implies a more even post-fisc distribution of income. Similarly, horizontal equity can be interpreted as requiring that individuals or families in similar economic positions receive the same gain or loss from redistribution.

Because the concept of equity has many dimensions, empirical estimates of the amount of redistribution must be interpreted carefully in order to avoid reaching misleading conclusions. Particular care is needed when those estimates are used to make intertemporal or interjurisdictional comparisons. Consider, for example, two societies where one has an equal distribution of neutral-fisc income and the other a very unequal distribution. Clearly the first society does not need a redistributional fiscal system. Assume that the members of the second society have a certain aversion to inequality and decide collectively to redistribute income through the fiscal system. Empirical studies would show redistribution in the second society and no redistribution in the first. To conclude from those results that the second society is more concerned about equity than the first would be erroneous. More meaningful information will be obtained if we compare, for each of the two societies, the degree of income inequality before and after the redistributional measures.

Such comparisons for Canada are provided in this chapter. They address the basic questions: how unequal is the distribution of income in Canada and how much is income inequality reduced by the Canadian fiscal system? After all, governments introduce redistributional measures because the existing degree of income inequality is considered to be socially unacceptable, as determined through the political process. As a first step we estimated the shares of income by six major income classes for each household type under the hypothetical case of a neutral fisc (equal to the pre-fisc) and the corresponding shares of post-fisc income. The results are shown in Table 4-1.

The last column of Table 4-1 shows that in the absence of fiscal redistribution the distribution of income for the entire population in 1986 would be quite unequal. The poor would have received only 4 percent of income although they represented 17.5 percent of the population and 21.6 percent of households. The rich, on the other hand, would have received 14.6 percent of income, over four times their share of population or households.

A general idea of the extent to which income inequality was reduced by fiscal redistribution in 1986 is provided by Table 4-2, which shows the difference between the post-fisc and neutral-fisc income shares. For all household types, with a minor exception in the case of singles, the difference is positive at the bottom half of the income scale (gainers) and negative at the top half (losers). The gain by the poor (5.33 percentage points) is almost equal to the loss to the high income class (5.29); similarly, the gain by the low income class (3.69) is slightly higher than the loss to the rich (3.07). Recall from Chapter 1 that total redistributional gains include the $20.5 billion deficit in 1986.

TABLE 4-1:   Share of Income and Population

	Singles	Single Parents	One-Income Families	Two-Income Families	Seniors	Total
	%	%	%	%	%	%
Poor						
Post fisc	2.1	1.4	1.9	1.0	2.9	9.3
Neutral fisc	1.1	0.4	0.9	0.6	1.1	4.0
Individuals	3.5	3.0	4.8	2.1	4.1	17.5
Households	7.5	2.5	3.1	1.3	7.1	21.6
Low income						
Post fisc	2.1	0.9	2.8	2.8	3.6	12.3
Neutral fisc	1.7	0.5	2.2	2.3	1.9	8.6
Individuals	2.4	1.3	5.2	5.0	4.0	17.9
Households	5.3	1.0	3.2	3.0	6.0	18.5
Lower-middle						
Post fisc	1.8	0.7	3.6	4.9	2.1	13.0
Neutral fisc	1.8	0.6	3.5	4.7	1.4	12.0
Individuals	1.6	0.9	5.5	7.4	1.7	17.1
Households	3.5	0.8	3.5	4.6	2.3	14.7
Upper-middle						
Post fisc	3.8	0.7	5.5	11.8	2.6	24.3
Neutral fisc	4.4	0.0	5.9	12.9	2.0	26.0
Individuals	2.6	0.7	6.2	13.8	1.6	25.0
Households	5.7	0.6	4.5	9.2	2.2	22.2
High income						
Post fisc	4.7	0.4	4.9	16.6	3.4	29.9
Neutral fisc	5.9	0.0	5.6	20.1	3.2	35.2
Individuals	2.1	0.2	3.2	12.3	1.5	19.3
Households	4.5	0.2	2.9	10.0	2.0	19.6
Rich						
Post fisc	1.1	0.0	3.2	5.4	1.4	11.2
Neutral fisc	1.4	0.0	4.1	7.1	1.6	14.2
Individuals	0.2	0.0	1.0	1.7	0.3	3.3
Households	0.5	0.0	0.8	1.5	0.4	3.3
All income classes						
Post fisc	15.5	4.1	22.0	42.5	15.9	100.0
Neutral fisc	16.4	0.0	22.2	47.7	11.2	100.0
Individuals	12.5	6.1	25.9	42.4	13.2	100.0
Households	26.9	5.2	18.1	29.7	20.1	100.0

TABLE 4-2: Change in Income Share Due to Fiscal Redistribution
Percentage Points

	Singles	Single Parents	One-Income Families	Two-Income Families	Seniors	Total
Poor	1.04	1.06	1.04	0.38	1.80	5.33
Low Income	0.39	0.36	0.62	0.53	1.78	3.69
Lower-Middle	-0.05	0.10	0.15	0.16	0.68	1.04
Upper-Middle	-0.68	-0.02	-0.41	-1.12	0.54	1.69
High Income	-1.22	-0.01	-0.75	-3.46	0.16	-5.29
Rich	-0.32	-0.01	-0.86	-1.67	-0.21	-3.07

The information contained in Table 4-1 is shown graphically by the Lorenz curve for the total population in Figure 4-1.[2] This curve is prepared by plotting the cumulative percentage of households along the horizontal axis and the corresponding cumulative percentage of income along the vertical axis. The diagonal line indicates a perfectly equal income distribution, as a given share of households receives an exactly equal share of income. The further away from the diagonal is the actual income distribution curve, the more unequal the income distribution is.

FIGURE 4-1: Lorenz Curves of Neutral-Fisc and Post-Fisc Income

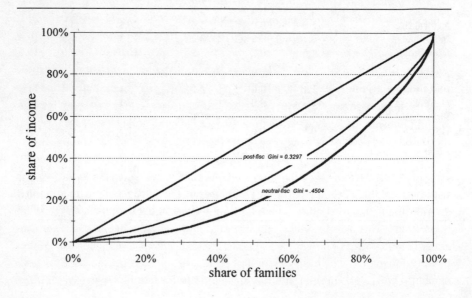

Figure 4-1 shows two Lorenz curves for the Canadian population. The curve labelled "post-fisc" shows the actual distribution of total post-fisc income, including the benefits of government expenditures minus the burden of taxation. The curve labelled "neutral-fisc" is associated with a fiscal regime that generates no income redistribution. This neutral-fisc concept assumes that the benefits and burdens of government fiscal policy are proportional to the distribution of private earnings adjusted for corporate taxes that are shifted back to labour and capital. The neutral-fisc curve, therefore, also represents the distribution of adjusted private earnings.

Figure 4-1 shows that the distribution of neutral-fisc income is quite unequal, as the associated Lorenz curve is considerably to the right of the diagonal. Figure 4-1 also shows that there is a substantial degree of fiscal redistribution, as the post-fisc Lorenz curve is located considerably to the left of its neutral-fisc counterpart.

A Lorenz curve can be transformed into a single index of income inequality, called the Gini coefficient after its originator. This index is calculated as the ratio of the area between the Lorenz curve and the diagonal to the total area on the right of the diagonal (half the area of the box). If there is perfect equality of income, the Lorenz curve is identical to the diagonal and the Gini coefficient equals 0; under complete inequality the Lorenz curve is identical to the horizontal axis (except at the 100 percent point) and the Gini coefficient equals 1.

Table 4-3 shows the estimated Gini coefficients for all households and for each of 15 household types under the neutral-fisc and post-fisc income concepts. *For all households, the Gini coefficient is 0.450 for neutral-fisc income. In the absence of fiscal redistribution, the distribution of income in Canada would be almost half way to complete inequality. The fisc reduces such inequality substantially; the Gini coefficient is lowered by more than one-quarter to 0.330.*

Table 4-3 also shows clear differences in the degree of inequality of neutral-fisc income among the 15 household types. Seniors and single-parent families have the highest degree of inequality with Gini values close to 0.5 for both groups. Among households headed by a senior, singles have the greatest income inequality (0.485) and couples with only one senior have the lowest (0.452). Among single-parent families inequality increases with the number of children; the Gini coefficient increases from 0.458 for families with one child to 0.477 and 0.476 for families with two and three or more children, respectively. The third most unequal income distribution is that of singles, which is slightly more equal than the average of all households. This is followed by one-income families, with Gini coefficients generally below 0.400. For this group, additional children are not associated with greater income inequality. The Gini coefficient increases for one-income couples with one child versus no children, it drops substantially for families with two children

TABLE 4-3:   Inequality and Redistribution by Household Type

		Gini Values	
Household Type	Neutral-Fisc	Post-Fisc	Change
Singles	.435	.298	-.138
Single parent			
1 child	.458	.240	-.218
2 children	.477	.185	-.292
3 or more children	.476	.114	-.363
Total	.465	.209	-.256
One-income family			
0 children	.395	.295	-.100
1 child	.405	.284	-.121
2 children	.335	.226	-.108
3 or more children	.359	.205	-.154
Total	.381	.265	-.117
Two-income family			
0 children	.298	.257	-.040
1 child	.274	.228	-.049
2 children	.271	.209	-.061
3 or more children	.278	.174	-.104
Total	.284	.225	-.059
Seniors			
Single	.485	.277	-.208
Two-senior couple	.471	.281	-.190
One-senior couple	.452	.298	-.154
Total	.514	.337	-.177
Total	.450	.330	-.121

and rises again for families with three or more children. Two-income families have the lowest degree of income inequality, with Gini coefficients below 0.300. Moreover, for this group inequality decreases for up to two children and then goes up again for three or more children.

Since redistributional policies are implemented for the purpose of reducing income inequality, one would expect that the extent to which the fiscal system reduced inequality would be positively related to the degree of inequality under the neutral-fisc situation. We tested this hypothesis by plotting the change in the Ginis against the respective neutral-fisc Ginis for the 15 household types. As shown in Figure 4-2, the two are positively related, as the observations fall on a positively-sloped line. The correlation between the two was found to be statistically significant at the 99 percent confidence level.

FIGURE 4-2:   Relationship Between Neutral-Fisc Inequality and
              Fiscal Redistribution

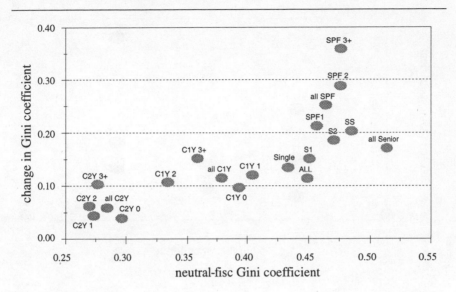

We conclude from the above discussion that the Canadian fiscal structure in 1986 reduced the degree of income inequality within each of the 15 household types. The reduction in inequality was greater for those households with a greater degree of inequality under the neutral fisc.

This positive relationship also holds with respect to the number of children by household type. As shown in Figure 4-3, for each household type, the degree of inequality reduction generally increases with the number of children. This result provides some indication that programs targeted to families with children have some effect in reducing overall income inequality.[3]

This differential degree of redistribution within household types does not automatically ensure a lower degree of inequality among household types. Consider the simple example where total households have been divided into two groups. Both groups have the same number of people and the same average income, however, group A has a more unequal distribution of income. We now introduce a transfer financed by a proportional tax on total income in group A and targeted to low income people in group A. The net result is a reduction in income inequality for group A and no change for group B. The overall degree of income inequality for the two groups combined is reduced, but the relationship between the two groups remains unchanged, as they continue to have equal average incomes.

FIGURE 4-3:   Fiscal Redistribution for Families with Children

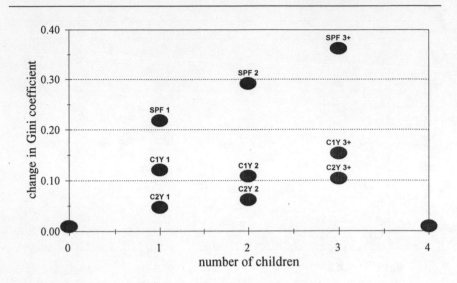

To show how fiscal redistribution affects the degree of inequality among different household types, we compared the average income of each household type with the relative change in its economic position produced by the fisc. The latter is measured by the ratio of a household type's share of post-fisc income to its share of neutral-fisc income.

As shown in Figure 4-4, when we order the 15 household types by average household income, the degree of fiscal redistribution falls as average income increases. The relationship between the two variables was found to be statistically significant at the 95 percent confidence level. As a result, *the degree of income inequality among household types is reduced by the fisc.* Another indication of this lower inter-group income inequality is provided by comparing the values of the Gini coefficient. The range of Ginis among household types is reduced from 0.214 to 0.184 by the fisc, indicating that fiscal redistribution tends to compress the distribution of average income by household type.

It should be stressed that in this chapter we have evaluated the relationship between redistribution and equity only with respect to one element of government activity, namely the fiscal system. Government also affects the well-being of Canadians through non-fiscal activities and through institutions that they do not control directly, but to which they have effectively delegated their power. These other "redistributional powers" include the conduct of monetary policy,

FIGURE 4-4: Relationship Between Average Income and Fiscal Redistribution

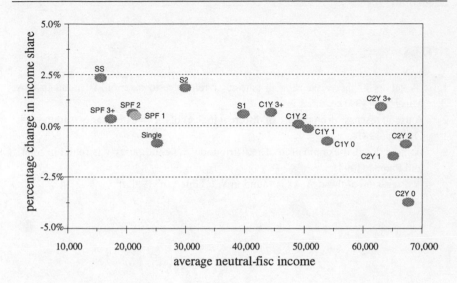

regulation of individual and business activities, competition policy, the administration of justice and the entire apparatus of property rights.

The fact that the redistribution generated by non-fiscal activities is very difficult to measure does not imply that its magnitude is insignificant or its direction progressive (pro-poor). Some economists have argued that the state's support for economic structures that promote wealth accumulation, which may generate increasing income inequality through time, is the most powerful redistributional policy and its effect is not in favour of the poor.[4] If, for a certain group, the non-fiscal activity of government generates redistribution equal in amount and opposite in direction to that produced by the fiscal system, the government has generated no net redistribution for that group. In that case one may argue that fiscal redistribution should be treated entirely as victim's compensation.

We acknowledge the above critique of fiscal redistribution studies. However, we believe that it is more useful to measure what we can rather than to give up because we can only obtain a partial measurement. Estimates of fiscal redistribution not only provide a useful basis for government policy, but also represent a benchmark for evaluating the magnitude of non-fiscal redistribution.

To summarize, this chapter has shown that in 1986 the Canadian fiscal system reduced considerably income inequality. Its redistributional impact within household types was higher for those types with the greatest degree of inequality of private earnings. Finally, it reduced the differences in average income among the household types.

NOTES

1.   A survey of these issues, with particular reference to taxation, is found in R.A. Musgrave (1993).
2.   A useful discussion on the use of different indices of income inequality is found in L. Osberg (1981).
3.   A more detailed examination of redistribution and child poverty is found in Sharif and Phipps (1994).
4.   A discussion of these views is found in W.I. Gillespie (1980*a*).

CHAPTER FIVE

Conclusions and Policy Directions

MAIN RESULTS

People often complain about the heavy burden of taxation, but seldom acknowledge the benefits they receive from government spending. This response may reflect the high visibility of taxation and the difficulty of measuring and allocating the benefits of public spending. It may also reflect the greater volume of published research on taxation. Without current estimates of the redistributional impact of all components of the fiscal system, taxation and government spending policy is made within an information vacuum. The last studies evaluating the full redistributional impact of the fisc in Canada were published nearly two decades ago and used data related to the early 1970s. This volume provides estimates of fiscal redistribution in Canada for 1986. We hope that the results will be of help in the analysis and design of fiscal and social policy.

Our findings challenge a number of traditional beliefs on the pattern of fiscal redistribution.

- In 1986, the Canadian fiscal system reduced substantially the degree of inequality in the distribution of income. Fiscal redistribution reduced the index of income inequality, the Gini coefficient, by 27 percent from 0.45 to 0.33.
- The degree of income inequality was reduced for each of 15 household types. The reduction in inequality was greatest for those households with the highest inequality of earnings.
- The fiscal system also reduced the degree of inequality among household types. The range of the Gini coefficients among household types was reduced by 14 percent from 0.21 to 0.18.
- Taxation was the most powerful tool of redistribution. This result is not affected by "less progressive" assumptions about the incidence of corporate

income taxes and real property taxes. The personal income tax is the major source of redistribution through taxation.

- Government purchases generated as much redistribution as transfer payments, primarily because of the progressive (pro-poor) distribution of health-care benefits.

- The provinces combined produced as much redistribution as the federal government, partly because they are responsible for delivering health care. The provincial tax system was also a strong source of redistribution, though not as strong as the federal one.

- Sales and excise taxes redistributed income from the middle class to the upper and lower income classes.

- Total redistribution, as measured by the sum of the gains received by those who benefited from the fiscal system, amounted to $58.4 billion. This is equivalent to 25 cents per dollar of government expenditures. The poor (those with income below 50 percent of the median) received 46 percent of this amount. The low income class (those with income between 50 percent and 75 percent of the median) received 34 percent. Each dollar of government spending provided 11 cents of redistribution in favour of the poor and another 8.5 cents in favour of the low income class.

- The middle class (those with income between 75 percent and 150 percent of the median) received substantial benefits from the fiscal system. Its gross gain amounted to $10.5 billion, equal to 40 percent of the gain by the poor. Within the middle class there was a transfer of $6.4 billion from non-senior upper middle class households to middle class seniors and lower middle class households.

- The middle class received 33.5 percent of transfer payments, almost equal to its share of households (36.9 percent).

- The fiscal system has varying impacts over the lifetime of individuals. Our results indicate that the Canadian fiscal system imposes penalties when individuals are in their labour attachment years, and therefore make labour supply decisions, and offers rewards after retirement from the labour force.

In interpreting these findings, however, it must be kept in mind that net redistribution included $20.5 billion of government deficit. The pattern of redistribution under a balanced budget cannot be determined *a priori*. An update of this study done after the federal budget is balanced would shed more light on this question. The use of actual post-fisc income, while allowing a comprehensive analysis of fiscal redistribution, involved some lack of precision in the allocation of the benefits of government purchases. Finally, the redistributional impact by order of government treats intergovernmental fiscal transfers as expenditures of the recipient and revenues of the donor government.

These findings shed some light on the functions of the fiscal system and its role in income redistribution. Government spending, and the taxation required to finance it, serve three main purposes:[1]

1. to supply public goods, such as national defence and the justice system, and social goods, such as health care and education.
2. to provide insurance against unforeseen fluctuations in the earnings of individuals and families during their lifetime.
3. to reduce the inequality of earnings by redistributing income from the rich to the poor.

Our results suggest that the Canadian fiscal system in 1986 was primarily directed at the first two objectives. A large portion of fiscal redistribution was the indirect (and unintended?) result of the provision of social goods, especially health care. Transfer payments involved programs with a large social insurance component, such as unemployment insurance benefits, old age security pensions, and pensions under the Canada/Quebec Pension Plan. The strict Robin Hood function of the fisc (a deliberate transfer of income from the rich to the poor) was limited relative to the other two.

In this chapter we interpret our findings in terms of alternative approaches to redistribution. We acknowledge that using results on fiscal redistribution for policy analysis is not an objective exercise, but involves subjective judgement with respect to both focus and prescription. Our focus is on exploring policy alternatives with the potential for delivering the existing degree of redistribution in a more efficient manner. We do not interpret the results as leading automatically to a prescription for less redistribution.

The empirical evidence that all three major components of the fiscal system — taxation, government purchases and transfer payments — generate redistribution in favour of lower income groups may tempt some readers to advocate a reduction in the degree of income redistribution. If equity is acquired at the expense of efficiency, it may be argued that a reduction in income redistribution would enhance economic efficiency. As pointed out by Okun (1975), however, "society can get more of two good things rather than sacrificing one for the other," by reducing inequalities of opportunities. We consider it more important to seek opportunities for breaking through the strict constraints of the equity-efficiency trade-off. To the extent that we exploit opportunities for improving the efficiency in the operation of both the public and private sectors, we may afford even more redistribution.

POLICY DIRECTIONS

The rest of this chapter evaluates two approaches to redistribution, called corrective redistribution and preventive redistribution. It presents a conceptual framework for policy analysis as a contribution to the debate on the future of redistribution policy in Canada with a view to improving both equity and efficiency.

Preventive versus Corrective Redistribution

These two approaches differ with respect to both main objectives and delivery mechanism.

Preventive redistribution involves policies that reduce inequalities of opportunities, thus generating a more level playing field and less disparity in private earnings. It is delivered primarily through the public provision of social goods and through non-fiscal instruments. Social goods include such goods and services as health care and education, which society considers of sufficient social importance to subsidize their prices as a means of increasing consumption, especially by those who could not otherwise afford them. Examples of non-fiscal instruments of preventive redistribution include the elimination of barriers to employment, an independent justice system, human rights legislation that prevents discrimination, active labour market policies, and legislation that curbs market power.

Corrective redistribution is aimed at reducing, *ex post*, socially unacceptable inequalities in private earnings. It is delivered largely through direct transfer payments to persons.

The two approaches also differ with respect to their implicit view of individual choices. Corrective redistribution views the problem largely as a matter of insufficient income for certain groups. The preferred solution is unconditional financial assistance, which does not interfere with individual choices. Preventive redistribution, on the other hand, aims at reducing inequality of opportunity. To that end it does not eschew interference with individual choice. It provides benefits only to the extent that individuals access the social goods and services subsidized by the government. It delivers redistribution to the extent that individuals engage in socially beneficial activity.

Since all redistribution measures have immediate impacts and dynamic effects through time, the separation between the two approaches is not water-tight. Reducing inequality of opportunity does not automatically assure equality of outcomes. Even over a lifetime, people's incomes will differ because of variations in human and non-human capital endowments, personal preferences and decisions, sheer luck or misfortune. At any point in time, some people are between jobs not by choice, others may be unable to participate in the labour market, others did not earn enough during their productive years to provide adequately for retirement. The effects of the above factors still need to be mitigated through corrective redistribution programs, which generally involve transfer payments to persons.

Because of the interactions between corrective and preventive redistribution, some policy instruments contain elements of both approaches. For example, progressive taxation acts as a tool of corrective redistribution as it lessens annual differences in earned income and therefore reduces annual income inequality. It is also an instrument of preventive redistribution to the extent that it reduces the potential for higher inequality in the distribution of wealth, thus generating some levelling of inequality of opportunities. A similar dual function may be performed by the Unemployment Insurance program. By providing income support to those who have lost their jobs, it may reduce the degree of inequality of annual income. To the extent that it improves job search efforts it may produce a better match between job seekers and employers and may contribute to less volatility in lifetime employment and earnings. Which of the two effects will prevail in the long run depends on the design of the program.

The foregoing discussion suggests that effective redistribution policy requires both approaches. The fundamental issue is the appropriate balance between the two. This is the subject of the following sections.

Corrective Redistribution

Our results show that the Canadian fiscal system uses both approaches, as it delivers redistribution through all three fiscal instruments. These instruments include the public provision of social goods, earlier identified as a major source of preventive redistribution. On the whole, however, Canadian redistribution policy appears to rely more heavily on the corrective approach. On the tax side, redistribution is delivered almost entirely through the progressive personal income tax system. This progressivity is often justified exclusively as a corrective measure. On the expenditure side, a large share is represented by transfer payments, the major instrument of corrective redistribution. They include programs strictly directed at redistribution — such as social assistance, the guaranteed income supplement, and income-tested credits — and transfers directed at the social insurance function — such as unemployment benefits, Old Age Security benefits, and pensions under the Canada/Quebec Pension Plan.

Heavy reliance on corrective redistribution is consistent with the traditional view of fiscal incidence. According to conventional wisdom, the tax system is roughly proportional and government purchases are not designed for redistributional purposes. Therefore, redistribution must be delivered primarily through transfer payments.[2] This approach rests on two fundamental assumptions: the efficient allocation of resources by a perfectly competitive market and the absence of perverse behavioural responses to transfer payments. We suggest in the following discussion that, when the above assumptions are relaxed, redistributional policy based primarily on the corrective approach may not be sustainable in the long run.

GENERAL ISSUES

The theoretical foundation of corrective redistribution, which assumes that markets behave according to the textbook model of competitive equilibrium and allocate resources in the most efficient manner, has come under increasing attack in the literature. Edmund Phelps (1994a), who synthesized a large body of research in his recent book *Structural Slumps*, shows that imperfections in labour markets, goods markets and credit markets lead to equilibria which are neither stable nor efficient. If the market does not yield an efficient equilibrium, then simply correcting, *ex post*, for socially unacceptable distributional outcomes still leaves an inefficient equilibrium. In such a situation, a direct attack on the forces that prevent the market from operating efficiently may be more fruitful.

In the labour market, imperfections arise because of changes in work effort partly caused by variations in the ratio of non-wage income to labour remuneration.[3] Non-labour income includes government transfers as well as private income from capital or from gifts and bequests. Increases in this ratio raise the cost of effective labour and lead to an inefficiently low equilibrium level of employment.[4] In the product market, imperfections arise because of the exercise of market power by firms as a result of less than perfect information on the part of customers. Since customers are viewed as assets generating a potential stream of purchases for an indefinite period of time, their present value is affected by changes in real interest rates. In setting its price, a firm is concerned not only with its immediate impact on current profits, but also with the contribution that an extra customer makes to the discounted present value of its expected stream of future profits. An increase in real interest rates reduces the present value of future customers, increases the exercise of market power, reduces the demand for labour and lowers equilibrium employment.

Phelps' analysis points out the fundamental shortcomings of corrective redistribution policies which are used as permanent solutions to structural market failures. Transfer payments provided as replacements for labour income raise the cost of effective labour and raise the equilibrium unemployment rate. If they result in a higher overall rate of consumption in the economy, they may put upward pressure on interest rates and further depress equilibrium employment and output. Therefore they not only have micro effects on the behaviour of the beneficiaries but macro effects on the performance of the economy. These negative effects are magnified when the transfers are financed by taxes, such as payroll taxes, which impose a relatively higher burden on wage than non-wage income. The equivalence of government transfers and non-wage income from private sources also highlights the shortcomings of policies that try to stimulate growth by increasing inequality in the distribution of wealth.

The shortcomings of heavy reliance on corrective redistribution can also be gleaned from models of endogenous growth and endogenous policy, such as that developed by Persson and Tabellini (1994). They develop an overlapping generations model in which individuals act both as economic agents and voters. As economic agents, individuals try to maximize the net return on their investment in human and non-human capital. As voters (represented by the median voter), they make voting decisions by comparing the marginal cost of redistribution with the marginal cost of the distortions caused by redistribution. According to Persson and Tabellini, economic growth depends both on the accumulation of human and non-human capital and on the political institutions and processes which translate conflicting interests into public policy decisions. In democratic societies with aversion to income inequality, economic structures which lead to increasing inequality of earnings would elicit strong redistributional policy responses. The political decisions would reduce the degree of private appropriation of economic returns, thus resulting in lower accumulation and lower growth. In their words, "The greater is income inequality, the lower is equilibrium growth" (p. 600).

The interaction between corrective redistribution and economic growth may have pernicious dynamic effects. As the degree of corrective redistribution increases to offset a rise in the inequality of earnings, so does the disincentive to work for benefit recipients, thus more people opt out of the labour force or reduce work effort. In either case there is a reduction in equilibrium employment. This, in turn, reduces the tax base for financing redistributive transfers. The resulting tax increases exacerbate the disincentives to work for those employed and paying taxes. This vicious circle may lead to what Persson and Tabellini call a "growth trap." Under certain conditions, "income inequality is or becomes so pronounced that it discourages further accumulation and growth" (p. 605).

SPECIFIC PROGRAMS

The shortcomings of corrective redistribution are evident in the failures of its major programs, such as social assistance and unemployment insurance.

Social Assistance is the program of last resort. It is administered by the provinces and territories, but is partly financed by the federal government through the Canada Assistance Plan. Canadians may be eligible for social assistance if their resources fall short of their needs as determined by a needs test. Social assistance rates differ among provinces and within each province with respect to factors such as family size, age of children, marital status and employability of the household head. Social assistance recipients may earn a certain amount of labour income without a reduction in their benefits. Any earnings in excess of the exempted amount reduce the amount of social assistance, in some provinces dollar per dollar.

The combination of benefit clawbacks, income-tested credits such as the GST and Child Tax Credit, and income and payroll taxes generates very high marginal tax rates on employment earnings for households on social assistance. This creates an employment wall which in some cases may be insurmountable. A study by Battle and Torjman (1994) shows that social assistance recipients in Ontario face marginal tax rate in the 80 to 95 percent range. If employment related expenses are added, the effective marginal tax rates may exceed 100 percent. Since they can only keep a minute share of their earnings from employment, social assistance recipients may not find employment an attractive alternative to welfare and cannot be expected to pursue actively employment opportunities. The welfare trap therefore can transform a temporary setback into a long-term withdrawal from productive activity. The higher taxes needed to finance the increased social assistance budget will reduce equilibrium employment and output.

The *Unemployment Insurance* program in its present form "is an unhappy compromise between ... the insurance and the income transfer models" (Corak 1994, pp. 152-153). This compromise reflects the view that unemployment has two major components: a cyclical component, resulting from fluctuations in economic activity, and a frictional/structural component, caused largely by imperfections in the labour and product markets. The insurance aspect addresses the cyclical component while the income transfer aspect deals with the frictional/structural component.

The verdict on the economic consequences of UI programs is not unanimous. Some authors argue that these programs introduce perverse incentives for both workers and employers. According to Snower (1994, p. 65), all unemployment benefit systems in OECD countries "tend to increase the unemployment whose effects they are meant to mitigate. The reasons are well-known: they push up wages (by improving workers' fall-back position in wage negotiations), and discourage job search (for when unemployed people find jobs, their unemployment benefits are withdrawn and they have to pay taxes)."[5] These effects, which compound existing labour market failures, are exacerbated when unemployment benefit schemes are financed through payroll taxes. Phelps (1994) found that increases in payroll taxes were a major source of the upward drift in the natural rate of unemployment in OECD countries. Empirical evidence points to a positive relationship between unemployment insurance schemes and the value of the non-accelerating inflation-rate of unemployment (NAIRU). For Canada, Fortin (1994) estimated that the expansion of the unemployment insurance program in 1971 raised the NAIRU by 1.3 percentage points; similarly the tightening of the program in 1977 and during 1990-94 reduced the NAIRU by 0.2 and 0.7 percentage points, respectively.

UI programs are designed to increase unemployment by allowing for longer job searches to gain a better job match. This expected increase in the NAIRU may be viewed as the cost that society is willing to pay for stabilizing the income of workers who are more susceptible to employment instability. However, if the program design introduces strong perverse incentives for both workers and employers, it may be argued that the cost is not minimized by the existing program.

There is some evidence that the Canadian UI system contains perverse incentives for both workers and employers. Green (1994, p.2) argues that "Canadian workers increasingly have tailored their labour supply behaviour to the characteristics of the UI system." The practice of laying people off subject to recall may be encouraged by the notion that labour compensation includes both wages and unemployment benefits (Corak 1994).

Arguments that the UI program produces excessive increases in unemployment are not universally accepted. Phipps (1993) suggests that claims about the disincentive effects of UI programs are exaggerated. Given the small wage elasticity of the labour supply, the labour supply response to perverse UI incentives may be negligible. Osberg (1993, p.16) points out that "the UI system not only contains disincentives to work ... it also contains incentives to *increased* labour supply." The latter would raise aggregate output.

Despite the lack of consensus on the economic consequences of UI programs, there is general agreement on the need to reform the existing UI system in Canada. As pointed out by Osberg (1993, p. 41), "any system which (as in 1992) spends $19.3 billion in benefits (plus $1.3 billion in administrative cost) and has 3.8 million claimants in a single year is sure to have lots of ways in which it can be improved." Improving the current UI is the stated objective of the federal government's comprehensive review for the purpose of reducing its disincentive effects (Canada 1994). This review has stimulated the search for solutions among academics and other non-government researchers. Recent suggestions for change are found in Courchene (1994), Green (1994), Lazar (1994) and Nakamura, Cragg and Sayers (1994).

EFFECTS ON THE DISADVANTAGED

Programs of corrective redistribution are strongly criticized by those who assume to be bearing most of the costs through taxation. As pointed out by Phelps (1994*b*), however, the biggest losers may be those targeted by the programs as beneficiaries. In Phelps' view "The welfare system harms disadvantaged workers through its impacts on the availability of jobs, on the overall reward from work, and on the morale of disadvantaged communities" (p. 54). When equilibrium unemployment is raised by the failures of corrective redistribution, the higher unemployment hits primarily the disadvantaged, because skilled and experienced workers may accept a lower paying job while waiting for a better opening. Disadvantaged workers also contribute, through compulsory payroll taxes and lower wages, to finance programs they may not be willing to buy, being too poor.

These negative effects of corrective redistribution on those it intends to assist may compound through time. As pointed out by Snower (1994, p. 65), the long-term unemployed miss the opportunity to acquire on-the-job skills; they also are more likely to face credit constraints, which further impairs their ability to acquire needed skills to compete effectively in the labour market. Long and frequent unemployment bouts and the substitution of government transfers for employment earnings may also devalue the importance of work for personal self-esteem, thus reducing morale and future job performance (Phelps 1994*b*, p. 55). In Phelps' view, the reduced attractiveness of work, in turn, is likely to create serious external diseconomies (harmful effects on society). First, the lack of jobs and relatively low wages may encourage the search for more rewarding criminal activities. Second, the availability of government support may foster a "culture of passivity" among the disadvantaged. These types of behaviour are capable of sapping the vitality of entire communities. A popular version of this view was presented recently in the cover story of *Business Week* (August 15, 1994), which provided examples of "how the growing gap between rich and poor is hurting the economy."

Some critics of corrective redistribution may suggest that the best solution to its shortcomings is the dismantling of the social safety net and a drastic reduction in the degree of redistribution. We interpret the surveyed literature to suggest that such a policy would be counterproductive. A more promising approach would involve a reform of the redistribution system aimed at reducing disincentives to productive activity. The potential benefits of this approach, which we have called preventive redistribution, are explored in the next section. In evaluating alternatives to corrective redistribution, we acknowledge that eliminating a disincentive to work does not create a job. The odds of a job seeker being offered a job are not improved by increasing his/her incentive to work. The reality of the situation is that the private sector can guarantee neither economic stability, nor permanently high employment rates, nor living wages for all workers. Therefore it is necessary to design mechanisms that shelter people from the unpredictable failures of the market without creating perverse incentives. The issue is not only the degree of government involvement in redistribution, but also the form of such involvement.

Preventive Redistribution

As mentioned earlier, preventive redistribution is aimed at reducing inequalities of opportunities, and is delivered through the public provision of social goods and the use of non-fiscal instruments. It is targeted to two main objectives:

1. The absence of wide and increasing disparities of earnings. In democratic societies, where citizens have a strong aversion to inequality, wide earnings disparities call forth redistributional adjustments that create obstacles to growth (Persson and Tabellini).
2. The maintenance of stable and low equilibrium rates of unemployment (Phelps).

The first objective can be pursued with the help of three general policy thrusts. The first involves an exploration of potential distortions arising from market power in the setting of executive pay. There is empirical evidence of a trend towards a widening gap between the earnings of employees at the top and bottom ends of the pay scale.[6] This polarization has been particularly pronounced in North America and may have been affected by the dramatic increases in the compensation of top executives. To the extent that exorbitant earnings incorporate the appropriation of economic rents from productivity increases, they introduce inefficiencies and generate barriers to employment creation. Lower employment, particularly among low income households, increases the cost of corrective government programs.

The second involves a review of the factors and policies that encourage the practice, prevalent but not confined to the early stages of an economic recovery, of using overtime as an alternative to new employment. Under this practice, which may be reinforced by provisions of the UI program, some workers make above-average earnings while others are denied the opportunity of steady employment and may become clients of corrective redistribution programs. This is another case where an optimizing private decision leads to increased social costs.

The third involves an attack on existing labour market rigidities. In an age of diverse family arrangements, lifelong learning and increased labour mobility, the efficient operation of labour markets requires very flexible working arrangements. These include, for example, job sharing, flexible work-weeks, less than full-time employment, periodic leaves and rotating assignments. Care should be taken, however, that the increased flexibility does not accelerate a change from perma-nent to casual jobs. As pointed out by Osberg (1994), such a change may lower labour earnings, reduce firms' incentives to train workers and lead to greater economic inequality and instability of earnings.

Even when direct government interference with the operation of the market creates efficiency costs, it may still be the best option. The alternative of correcting the socially-unacceptable outcomes of market decisions may generate greater economic inefficiencies. In comparing corrective and preventive redistribution, "it would be useful to compare the marginal cost of policies which simply compensate for the inequality in the distribution of private earnings with the marginal cost of policies that are directed at reducing the inequality of private earnings." (Dahlby and Ruggeri 1995).

Phelps' analysis suggests three general policies for maintaining stable and high rates of employment. The first involves a reduction in real interest rates. High interest rates raise unemployment through two channels. They increase non-wage income, thus bolstering workers' willingness to quit or to shirk and raising the cost of effective labour. They also depress the present value of assets. If workers are treated as assets, a reduction in their present value lowers the demand for labour. Similarly, if customers are viewed as assets, a reduction in the present value of future customers increases the firm's exercise of market power and reduces employment and output.

In Phelps' view, real interest rates are directly affected by the government's spending policy. Permanent increases in public consumption, even when financed by taxation, tend to raise their value. The increase in interest rates will be higher if public consumption is financed through borrowing. Government policies that avoid deficit financing, except as a temporary countercyclical measure, and reduce public debt would raise equilibrium employment. The importance of reducing real interest rates and eliminating government deficits as instruments for renewed economic growth and high employment are also stressed by Baily, Burtless and Litan (1993).

Second, stability of employment would be enhanced by the avoidance of policies that amplify the magnitude of cyclical fluctuations. Empirical evidence suggests that the effect of a cyclical downturn on unemployment extends well beyond the duration of the downturn. A study by James (1991) shows that the persistence of high unemployment rates in the 1980s was largely caused by the "duration effects" of the 1981-82 recession.

Third, equilibrium unemployment can be reduced by a change in the composition of public spending away from consumption and towards investment goods. Such a shift reduces any potential crowding out of consumer demand, raises the real price of capital goods and stimulates labour demand, by reducing the relative price of labour, and in so doing reduces real interest rates. Unemployment equilibrium is also reduced if the government engages in the supply of labour-intensive services. In addition to adding directly to employment, they generate a positive distributional effect. Since there is less polarization of earnings in the public than in the private sector, public employment lowers the degree of inequality of private earnings thus reducing the need for corrective measures.

Fourth, equilibrium unemployment can be reduced by a change in the tax mix that reduces the role of payroll taxes. These taxes impose a differential burden on wage income relative to non-wage income (including income from capital). In Phelps' view, a proportional income tax — a flat tax rate on both wage and non-wage income — is more efficient than a proportional payroll tax because it may have little effect on the incentive wage at a given unemployment rate. The payroll tax, as well as the wage component of the income tax, raises the efficiency wage when the worker compares the value of having or not having a job. The tax on non-wage income under the flat income tax, however, lowers the efficiency wage because it reduces the value of not having a job.

Phelps' structural analysis provides an efficiency argument for wealth taxes or progressive income taxes. The accumulation of wealth increases equilibrium unemployment if it results in an increasing ratio of non-wage to wage income because it provides incentives for detachment from the labour force and increased shirking. These negative effects are eliminated if income from capital is reinvested in a manner that does not provide income that can be used as an alternative to wages. Such an outcome would result if the government appropriated it and then invested it directly, or indirectly by providing firms with investment tax credits. If income from wealth is positively associated with total income, a progressive income tax may be as effective as, and simpler than, a wealth tax.

Since policy-induced structural changes are expected to have permanent effects, their influence is not confined to a single generation. The evaluation of the intergenerational implications of structural policies should be a fruitful area of policy analysis. Pioneered by Kotlikoff (1992), "generational accounting" offers special insights unavailable from impact studies. An important area of study for redistributional policy is the effect of policy on the bequest motive and the behavioural response of both donor and recipient across generations.

The structuralist analysis also leads to specific policy suggestions to stimulate incentives to work and raise the living standards of low-wage workers. Some authors favour employment subsidies as an alternative to unconditional transfers. The former can be considered empowering transfers, as they increase the potential for higher labour earnings, as opposed to the unempowering nature of the latter (Dahlby and Ruggeri 1995).

Phelps (1994) has proposed a scheme that would provide "a subsidy to every qualifying firm based on the stock of low wage workers on its rolls, in order to pull up the wage rates and employment rates of all very disadvantaged workers"

(p. 56). This program would be financed by savings in welfare costs, unemployment payments, crimefighting and increased tax revenue.

Fitoussi (1994) suggests a combination of legislated minimum wages and wage subsidies. In his research using data for France, he found that strict minimum wage legislation raises unemployment among young unskilled workers but has little effect on overall unemployment. The obvious solution to him is complementing minimum wage legislation with wage subsidies to firms that employ young unskilled workers.

Snower (1994) has proposed what he calls a benefit-transfer program which would allow the long-term unemployed "to use part of their unemployment benefits to provide vouchers to firms that hire them." This proposal would transform unemployment benefits into employment subsidies. The difference between the wage paid by a firm and the net income received by the worker measures the value of the employment subsidy.

Various wage subsidies schemes have been tried in different countries, with varying degrees of success (Iacobacci and Grignon 1993). In Canada, an employment tax credit was available during the 1978-81 period and a scheme exempting small firms from the increase in UI contribution if they hired new workers was introduced in 1993. In the United States a tax credit for the employment of disadvantaged groups was introduced in 1979. Variations of Snower's proposal have been implemented in the UK and Australia.

A structuralist approach would also support active labour market policies because they reduce labour market imperfections. A survey of European unemployment insurance schemes by Gross (1994) yielded the conclusion that active labour market policies can be effective. After reviewing the European experience during the 1980s, she concluded that targeted active policies — such as continuous help throughout the job search — did reduce the duration of unemployment.

Another avenue for structural policy is training and skill upgrading. Although the debate on the effectiveness of direct government delivery of training is not settled (Lazar 1994), there is general agreement that increases in human capital, especially for those with low skills, will increase employment and social welfare and reduce the need for corrective redistribution. Baily, Burtless and Litan (1993) consider government policy aimed at boosting investment in worker training as a cornerstone of their program for "growth with equity." In their view, "the most effective way of reducing earnings inequality is to increase the relative skills of those now at the bottom of the wage and skill distribution."

These policy suggestions are not presented as ready-made recipes for automatic implementation in Canada. They provide a different way of thinking about employment and redistribution policy which may be worth pursuing. They share a belief in the need "for creating institutions to enlist the self-help of the disadvantaged by raising the reward to their initiative and perseverance in gaining employment" (Phelps, 1994b). They also share the belief that government should be actively involved in this process, rather than simply providing financial support to those discarded, temporarily or permanently, from the labour market. This new way of thinking involves a reorientation of redistributional policy from passive social policy to "programs for economic justice," by which Phelps means government policy that ensures employment and fair wages even for the least skilled workers. Phelps' dichotomy between programs of social justice and economic justice is parallelled in our distinction between corrective and preventive redistribution.

Concluding Comments

A comparison between corrective and preventive redistribution can be illustrated using the familiar "production possibility frontier" shown in Figure 5-1. The horizontal axis measures amounts of one good (equity), while the vertical axis measures the other good (efficiency) (Osberg 1993). This figure conveys the concept of trade-offs with respect to redistribution policy: a reduction in income inequality necessarily exacts a price in terms of economic efficiency. The conclusion applies only in the case of corrective redistribution, which usually confines policy to movements along the production possibility frontier, say from A to B, with greater equity involving lower efficiency. As argued in the previous section, there is the danger that over time corrective redistribution may involve a move from A to C, thus yielding lower efficiency for the same degree of equity, or even from A to D, with lower efficiency and less equity.

In a second-best world — where production, distribution and redistribution are beset by inefficiencies — the economy operates inside the production possibility frontier, such as point D. In this case, it may be possible to design policies that generate a movement from D towards A, yielding more of both equity and efficiency. We have called this approach preventive redistribution.

The persistence of high deficits and the relentless expansion of the national debt has forced Canadian governments to redesign their policies with the overall objective of moving towards balanced budgets. The policy debate makes it clear that the status quo is not an option. Redistribution policy heavily reliant on the corrective approach has been tried and found wanting. The opportunity has risen for a paradigm shift and a change of direction. We suggest that consideration should be given to a new balance in redistribution policy which places primary emphasis on the preventive approach, leaving the corrective approach in a supporting role.

FIGURE 5-1: The Equity-Efficiency Trade-off in Redistribution

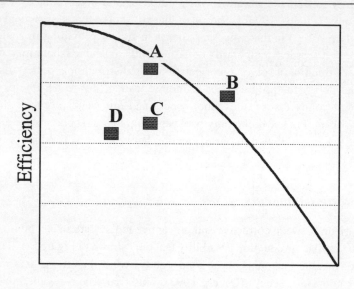

Equity

A comprehensive program which attempts to break through the traditional equity-efficiency trade-off has been developed for the United States by Baily, Burtless and Litan (1993). Their program includes measures aimed exclusively at stimulating economic growth, measures directed at reducing income inequality and measures aimed simultaneously at both. The last category includes policies that possess the characteristics of preventive redistribution measures. They include the improvement of skill training in schools, the establishment of national apprenticeship programs for workers with less than college education, improved R&D programs for public training efforts and the upgrading of national and state employment services.

It should be stressed that a policy that makes prevention of wide and increasing income disparities the cornerstone of redistribution does not necessarily imply either a larger or a smaller government. It does imply, however, a different role for government. It requires active policy aimed at preventing wide disparities in opportunities and outcomes, not just the passive policy of providing a safety net. It requires active government involvement, though not direct public delivery, in employment policy, training and other policies that promote high employment, rather than simply providing a minimum standard of living to those dropped by the market. Ultimately, it involves a shift of primary emphasis from passive social policy to active economic policy.

In developing a new paradigm for redistribution policy we suggest a careful evaluation of the following areas:

1. *Government spending on social goods, such as health care and education.* Our results show that such spending, especially spending on health care, generates a considerable amount of fiscal redistribution. These two areas of public spending help provide a more level playing field and strengthen equality of opportunity. In this case, redistribution catches a free ride on the decision to provide social goods and causes no additional cost. The potential efficiency costs of redistribution can be reduced by exploiting opportunities for complementarity between public purchases and redistribution. In reforming the health-care delivery system to improve its efficiency, care should be taken not to impair universal accessibility or reduce coverage for the disadvantaged, so as not to create barriers to their ability to earn a living. In primary and secondary education, it may be helpful to provide properly structured programs that teach employment skills to students who are not academically inclined. Postsecondary education also may benefit from having programs designed cooperatively with industry and from strengthening, where feasible, the links between formal education and on-the-job training. Care should be taken to ensure that the financing of education does not increase the relative price of acquiring human capital.

2. *Active involvement in reducing market imperfections.* Structuralist analysis suggests that major efficiency gains may be obtained from policies that improve the operation of both the labour and product markets. Two areas seem to offer good potential for efficiency gains. The first involves institutional changes that improve coordination between government, labour and business. The second involves the use of tax policy instruments to reduce disincentives to work and prevent the appropriation of rents.

3. *Active labour market policies.* Efficiency improvements can be gained by a shift from providing income support for unemployment to subsidizing employment. Government support for training, skill-upgrading and job search should also be beneficial.

4. *Intergenerational issues.* Policies designed to offset temporary market failures or to counteract short-term economic fluctuations need not address intergenerational effects. Structural policies aimed at permanent adjustments cannot ignore them. A new paradigm in redistribution policy will lead to more effective programs if policy design takes explicit account of intergenerational effects.

Although the new paradigm involves a shift of emphasis from corrective to preventive approaches to redistribution, it still involves the use of all three major instruments of redistribution. What is altered is the relative role of each instrument. Progressive taxation will continue to serve the purpose of preventing widening disparities in the distribution of wealth, which are capable of generating increasing inequality of income. The role of government spending on social goods, especially health care and education, is enhanced. There is also a strengthening of government non-fiscal instruments. Together they provide a more level playing field, help maintain high levels of employment, and offer a framework where people can provide for their needs through their own efforts throughout their lives.

Transfer payments will still remain the main instrument of corrective redistribution, but their role would be substantially reduced. They will be better focused to provide a true, and temporary, safety net. The social insurance function of government would be reduced by structural policies that maintain higher and more stable levels of equilibrium employment. The objectives of this function need to be reviewed for the purpose of minimizing efficiency costs. In this respect, it may be useful to review policies that, in the process of stabilizing income during a person's lifetime, impose penalties during the working years.

NOTES

1. Stabilization of incomes and the price level policies influencing the balance of payments, trade policy, and providing for an appropriate rate of savings are also important functions of fiscal policy, as pointed out by Musgrave, Musgrave and Bird (1987, pp. 13-15). The above policies may have distributional consequences, but are beyond the focus of this study on fiscal redistribution through the budget.
2. See the survey of studies in Chapter 1.
3. See, for example, Phelps (1968), Stiglitz (1974), Solop (1979), Calvo (1979), Layard and Nickell (1987), Greenwald and Stiglitz (1988).
4. Similar structuralist conclusions may be derived from a model of the labour market that incorporates transaction externalities (the so-called "thin market externality") in the cost of matching by unemployed workers and firms with vacancies. As Diamond (1981, 1984), Howitt (1983), Howitt and MacAfee (1987) and Pissarides (1990) have shown, the economy may become stuck at an inefficient low employment equilibrium. Van Wart (1994) has shown that the "thin market externality" can generate a permanent shift in the rate of equilibrium unemployment in response to temporary or cyclical shocks in the unemployment rate.
5. Evidence of the disincentive effects of the Canadian UI program is found in Green (1994), Millbourne, Purvis and Schoones (1991), Card and Riddell (1993), Corak (1993).
6. See, for example, Levy and Murnane (1992).

Postscript

FISCAL CHANGES SINCE 1986

The Canadian fiscal system has changed since 1986 as a result of budgetary measures by all orders of government. This postscript identifies the major changes and evaluates the likely direction of thier redistributional impact. We conclude that these changes have not significantly altered the fiscal incidence results presented for 1986.

Taxes

There have been a number of discretionary tax changes since 1986 which may have altered the degree to which the Canadian fiscal system redistributes income. These include partial de-indexation of the personal income tax, federal income and sales tax reforms, adjustments to provincial tax rates and bases, and the introduction of provincial payroll taxes.

FEDERAL

Prior to 1986, the PIT was fully indexed for the effects of nominal increases in incomes through annual adjustments to both the rates and thresholds. In 1986 the federal government removed indexation for the first 3 percent of Consumer Price Index increases. This allows effective PIT rates to rise each year by treating inflation up to 3 percent as an increase in real income.

The federal tax reforms of 1988 and 1991 altered, in particular, the personal income tax and the federal sales tax. The key elements of the 1988 PIT reform reduced the number of tax brackets from ten to three, reduced the number of surtaxes from three to one, reduced the statutory top marginal tax rate from 34 to 29 percent, converted personal exemptions and most deductions into non-refundable tax credits at a fixed 17-percent rate, reduced the dividend gross-up and tax credit, increased the inclusion rate for capital gains, and eliminated forward-averaging of income. An additional PIT high income surtax was imposed the next year.

The Corporate Income Tax reform included the reduction in the tax rates for general, small business and manufacturing income. The inclusion rate for capital gains was increased to 75 percent from 50 percent for both individuals and corporations. There was a substantial overall reduction in specific tax preferences, such as investment tax credits and borrowing costs deductions. Several studies concluded that the overall effective CIT rate was increased as the result of the combination of these changes.[1]

Federal sales tax reform replaced the Manufacturers' Sales Tax with a consumption type value-added tax, the Goods and Services Tax, in 1991. The key elements of federal sales tax reform were the imposition of the tax on the final consumer, rather than the manufacturers and wholesalers, the general expansion of input tax credits to eliminate tax on business inputs and exports, a broadening of the base to include most goods and services and enhancement of the sales tax credit, which is a direct transfer to persons.

Federal payroll taxes underwent less structural change. The employees' portion of the UI premium increased from 2.35 percent of employment income in 1986 to 3 percent in 1993, and the maximum employee portion of the premiums increased from $605 to $1,162. The CPP premium rate increased from 1.8 percent of employment income to 2.5 percent, and the maximum employee portion of the premium increased from $419 to $752. In both years the CPP premium was payable on employment income in excess of 10 percent of the yearly maximum pensionable earnings up to the maximum pensionable earnings. The UI premium was payable on all employment earnings up to the maximum annual insurable earnings.

PROVINCIAL

Federal de-indexation of the personal income tax also served to increase effective provincial PIT rates, which are based on basic federal tax. Provincial basic PIT rates increased in all provinces, except Alberta, from 1986 to 1994 and surtaxes were introduced or increased in British Columbia, Saskatchewan, Ontario, Quebec, Nova Scotia and P.E.I. Tax reductions for low-income earners were increased in Alberta, Ontario, Saskatchewan and Quebec.

Provinces generally have raised consumption taxes since 1986. Four provinces have raised their retail sales tax rates — Saskatchewan, Manitoba, Ontario and Nova Scotia. Quebec harmonized its PST with the federal GST between 1992 and 1994, broadening the base and increasing the effective tax rate. Other provinces expanded their PST bases over the period to include some services and provide fewer exemptions, except for Alberta, which still has no general sales tax. Fuel tax rates have been raised in every province, with an unweighted average increase of the nominal per unit rate of about 50 percent. After adjusting for inflation, most provincial rates are up by an average of about 13 percent. Tobacco tax rates rose rapidly until 1994. From 1986 until February 1994, inflation-adjusted per unit rates rose in every province, by an average of about 50 percent. Large to-bacco tax reductions were coordinated by the federal government in early 1994, resulting in dramatic tax cuts in five eastern provinces. The nominal rates were reduced to below the 1986 rates in Ontario, Quebec, New Brunswick and Nova Scotia. On average, real tobacco tax rates are about the same as 1986, but with a greater variation among provinces.

There has been little change in provincial corporate income tax, capital tax or insurance premiums tax rates. There has been an increase in the number of prov-inces providing a special rate for manufacturing and processing corporations under the CIT and in the number of provinces imposing a special capital tax on financial institutions. General provincial payroll taxes are now imposed in four provinces (Quebec, Manitoba, Ontario, Newfoundland), with Ontario's replacing the health-care premium and Newfoundland's replacing a local poll tax. These payroll taxes and the health-care premiums in British Columbia and Alberta have all had rate increases and the bases have been generally broadened.

TAX SHARES AND TOTAL TAX BURDEN

These discretionary changes are not the only sources of changes in the tax mix since 1986. The major change affecting the relative tax mix and the overall tax burden has been the rapid growth in PIT revenues as a result of its progressive rate structure, assisted by partial de-indexation. In addition, CIT revenues have been affected by lower taxable corporate profits over the 1986 to 1994 period. Corporate profits nationally fell sharply during the 1991-92 recession, then rose back close to the 1986 real levels by 1994. However, losses incurred during the recession are still being carried forward, reducing taxable corporate income for 1994 (Statistics Canada 1995).

Table 1 shows the combined federal-provincial tax revenues for 1986 and 1994 (unadjusted System of National Accounts [SNA] basis), and the changes in the shares of each tax source. Changes in the shares of the different taxes have been

TABLE 1: Total Government Revenue from Taxation, 1986 and 1994
(Excluding Non-Residents)

	1986			1994		
	$ million	% Share	% of GDP	$ million	% Share	% of GDP
Direct taxes on persons						
Personal income tax	62,378	37.5	12.3	104,277	38.6	13.9
Contributions to UI	9,615	5.8	1.9	19,940	7.4	2.7
Contributions to CPP/QPP	6,246	3.8	1.2	12,931	4.8	1.7
Contributions to WCB	3,224	1.9	0.6	4,290	1.6	0.6
Estate taxes	13	0.0	0.0	2	0.0	0.0
Subtotal	81,476	48.9	16.1	141,440	52.3	18.9
Direct taxes on corporations						
Corporate income tax	14,081	8.5	2.8	16,882	6.2	2.3
Other corporate taxes	55	0.0	0.0	174	0.1	0.0
Subtotal	14,136	8.5	2.8	17,056	6.3	2.3
Indirect taxes						
General sales taxes*	23,699	14.2	4.7	39,138	14.5	5.2
Fuel taxes*	4,523	2.7	0.9	9,466	3.5	1.3
Other excise taxes and duties*	5,838	3.5	1.2	6,276	2.3	0.8
Customs import duties	4,169	2.5	0.8	3,765	1.4	0.5
Liquor profits	2,149	1.3	0.4	2,474	0.9	0.3
Capital tax	1,275	0.8	0.3	2,665	1.0	0.4
Real property tax	15,695	9.4	3.1	28,596	10.6	3.8
Miscellaneous	3,430	2.1	0.7	4,161	1.5	0.6
Subtotal	60,778	36.5	12.0	96,541	35.7	12.9
Natural resource revenue	4,865	2.9	1.0	5,936	2.2	0.8
Other revenue						
Provincial payroll taxes	1,796	1.1	0.4	4,169	1.5	0.6
Health insurance premiums	2,229	1.3	0.4	1,367	0.5	0.2
Motor vehicle lics. & reg.	1,601	1.0	0.3	2,676	1.0	0.4
Fees and charges	598	0.4	0.1	952	0.4	0.1
Subtotal	6,224	3.7	1.2	9,164	3.4	1.2
Hospital revenue	101	0.1	0.0	192	0.1	0.0
*Total tax revenue***	*166,538*	*100.0*	*32.9*	*270,329*	*100.0*	*36.0*

Notes:
*The excise tax breakdown uses adjusted FMS amounts. FMS amounts for 1994 are based on 1993-94 fiscal year and the growth from 1992-93. Total excise taxes are the SNA amounts.
**Total does not include contributions to public pensions and lottery revenue.

small. The ratio of PIT to total taxes increased from 37.5 percent to 38.6 percent. The biggest changes in relative tax shares has been the increase in federal payroll taxes (UI and CPP/QPP premiums) from 9.5 percent to 12.2 percent and the decline of the CIT from 8.5 percent to 6.2 percent.

Table 1 also shows that Canadian taxes have increased from 32.9 percent of Gross Domestic Product (GDP) in 1986 to 36 percent in 1994 (measured on the SNA basis). Personal income taxes have increased from 12.3 percent to 13.9 percent of GDP, social insurance payroll taxes (UI, CPP/QPP, WCB premiums) have increased from 3.8 percent to 5 percent of GDP, and property taxes have increased from 3.1 percent to 3.8 percent of GDP. On the other hand, combined corporate income and capital taxes have decreased from 3 percent to 2.6 percent of GDP between 1986 and 1994.

Purchases

FEDERAL

Direct federal purchases involve primarily public good type of expenditures, such as protection of personal and property and general government. Although the federal government affects provincial spending through intergovernmental transfers, such as those for health care and postsecondary education, this effect is not measured separately in our study because actual spending is assigned to each order of government.

Federal direct spending for the provision of goods and services has fallen as a share of total spending and as a proportion of GDP between 1986 and 1994. This is indicated on Table 2, where federal purchases are the largest component of other current expenditures on goods and services. This is partly the result of the increase in the interest payments on the public debt. Table 2 indicates that combined federal and provincial interest payments have increased only very slightly as a proportion of total spending. However, the federal share of the total debt increased from about 50 percent to almost 60 percent.

PROVINCIAL

Recent provincial policy on the provision of goods and services has been largely directed at controlling the growth of health care and education costs. Most provinces have moved to de-insure various medical services from the national medicare program, to shorten hospital stays, reduce the number of hospital beds and to reduce the number of hospital employees. At the same time, there has been

TABLE 2:   Total Government Expenditure, 1986 and 1994
(Excluding Non-Residents)

	1986			1994		
	$ million	% Share	% of GDP	$ million	% Share	% of GDP
Current expenditure on goods and services						
Health*	29,735	13.6	5.9	48,425	14.0	6.5
Education*	28,808	13.2	5.7	44,537	12.9	5.9
Other*	46,369	21.2	9.2	64,248	18.6	8.6
Subtotal**	104,911	48.0	20.7	157,209	45.6	21.0
Transfer payments to persons						
Unemployment Insurance	10,394	4.8	2.1	15,012	4.4	2.0
Canada/Quebec Pension Plan	7,422	3.4	1.5	19,688	5.7	2.6
Old Age Security	13,148	6.0	2.6	20,170	5.8	2.7
Direct social assistance	6,280	2.9	1.2	14,812	4.3	2.0
Other	19,570	9.0	3.9	37,041	10.7	4.9
Subtotal**	56,814	26.0	11.2	106,723	31.0	14.2
Transfer payments to business	14,119	6.5	2.8	12,335	3.6	1.6
Interest on the public debt	42,754	19.6	8.5	68,556	19.9	9.1
Total expenditure	*218,598*	*100.0*	*43.2*	*344,823*	*100.0*	*46.0*

Notes:
* Health and Education are adjusted FMS amounts. FMS amounts for 1994 are based on 1993-94 fiscal year and the growth from 1992-93. Other is a residual category from the SNA total.
**Grants to postsecondary educational institutions have been deleted from *Transfers to persons* and added to *Current expenditure on goods and services.*

enhancement in the provision of homecare services and in certain types of preventive health programs.

The demographic cost pressures have not been as great in education. Enrolment in elementary and secondary education has been essentially flat over the period, while that for postsecondary has continued to increase (see Ruggeri and Hermanutz 1995). Real spending per pupil for elementary and secondary schooling rose by about 20 percent from 1986 to 1992, but we would expect that this trend has slowed or reversed in recent years. Real per pupil spending on postsecondary education was essentially constant between 1986 and 1992, but this level was down significantly from per pupil spending in the 1970s and early 1980s.

Despite the perception of a deep retrenchment in provincial spending on health care and education, both of these major components of provincial spending have increased as a share of total government expenditures and in relation to GDP, as shown in Table 2. Relative to GDP, spending on health has increased from 5.9 percent in 1986 to 6.5 percent in 1994, while that for education has grown only slightly. These changes are largely demographically driven, while discretionary policy has attempted in recent years to reduce this growth.

Transfers

FEDERAL

Three major initiatives altered federal transfer programs between 1986 and 1994. The clawback of OAS through a special income surtax for seniors with high incomes was introduced in 1989, followed by the income-testing of the age deduction from the PIT in 1994 (which can be considered a transfer payment delivered through the tax system). In 1993 the Family Allowance and the dependent credit from PIT were eliminated and repackaged into an enriched Child Tax Benefit, which is income tested.

Unemployment Insurance benefits were reduced and retargeted in several initiatives. The minimum qualifying period was increased in 1990 and again in 1994 (from 8 to 12 weeks in the regions with the highest unemployment rate); the benefit rate was reduced in 1993 and in 1994 from 60 percent to a split benefit rate of 60 percent for those with earnings below $390/week or with dependents and 55 percent for all others; the maximum duration of benefits was reduced slightly in 1990; finally, benefits were denied to those who quit their jobs without just cause and those who were fired in 1993.

PROVINCIAL

Provincial expenditures include a much smaller share of transfers to persons than do federal expenditures. Although there are a number of smaller transfer programs that vary by province, the major provincial transfers are social assistance payments. Provinces have been experimenting with a large number of structural changes in social assistance over this period. Some of these changes were designed to address problems of work disincentive, welfare dependence and the growth in the proportion of very young recipients. There has also been a general retargeting of benefits from single "employables" without children to more stringently-defined unemployables and persons with dependent children.

Over the period from 1985 to 1992, Ontario and Alberta increased their social assistance benefit expenditures per recipient substantially and Newfoundland, Nova

Scotia, P.E.I., Quebec and Manitoba all increased real benefits. British Columbia and New Brunswick maintained benefits roughly constant over the period, while Saskatchewan reduced benefits. The number of recipients and cases were up in all provinces over this period (see Inventory of Social Security Programs in Canada 1987 and 1993). Since 1992, Alberta and P.E.I. have reduced individual and family benefits significantly, Manitoba, Saskatchewan and New Brunswick have reduced average benefits somewhat, and British Columbia, Quebec and Nova Scotia have raised average benefits. Ontario's benefit rate continued to increase at a slower pace, but this trend has been recently reversed. The recession of 1991-92 raised the number of social assistance recipients in all provinces, especially in Ontario, and most provinces have since then been attempting to, more or less aggressively, reduce caseloads rather than implementing major cuts to benefit rates. Table 2 indicates that spending on social assistance has grown from 1986 to 1994, both as a share of total government spending (from 2.9 percent to 4.3 percent) and of GDP (1.2 percent to 2 percent).

REDISTRIBUTIONAL IMPACT

Taxes

FEDERAL

The federal tax revenue structure is dominated by the personal income tax (PIT). In 1994-95 revenue from the PIT represented nearly 50 percent of total federal tax revenue. Since the PIT is the only progressive component of the federal tax system, its relative importance in the federal revenue structure would automatically increase through time because its revenue would grow faster than that of other taxes. As a result, in the absence of discretionary tax changes, the progressivity of the federal tax system would tend to increase, though very slowly. A number of tax changes since 1986 may have halted this trend and perhaps temporarily reversed it.

The first major change was the partial de-indexation of the PIT, introduced in 1986. Since its effects are cumulative from one year to the other, the magnitude of its impact upon PIT progressivity increases through time. As pointed out by Ruggeri, Van Wart and Howard (1994a), by itself partial de-indexation "raises effective tax rates of lower income classes by a greater proportion than higher income classes and leads to a redistribution of after tax real income from low to high income classes." They concluded that "in the absence of discretionary adjustments to statutory tax rates and/or tax brackets, the degree of progressivity of the PIT will continue to be eroded through time, causing the personal income tax to regress towards proportionality."

A reduction in progressivity was also caused by the personal income tax reform of 1988. Van Wart and Ruggeri (1991) analyzed the effects of the 1988 income tax reform on the progressivity of the PIT and the distribution of income. They concluded that "overall, PIT reform redistributed the share of after-tax income from low income to high income classes." They argue that the magnitude of this redistribution may increase through time. In their view, "the provision of greater incentive for work effort and saving by the rich and lower incentives for the poor, together with greater progressivity PIT for the middle class and lower progressivity for the rich, may lead through time to increasing inequality of wealth between lower and upper income Canadians."

Another major tax change which tended to reduce the overall progressivity of the federal tax system was the substantial increase in the rates of the Manufacturers' Sales Tax (MST). This tax has generally been found to be regressive over most of the income distribution (see, for example, Ruggeri and Bluck 1992). Consumers at the low end of the income scale were partly sheltered form the burden of the MST through two channels. First, some government transfers, which represent a large share of their income, are indexed for increases in consumer prices and, therefore, automatically offset the increased tax burden by raising the amount of those transfers. Second, the government enriched the sales tax credit for low income Canadians. Even with these adjustments, the increased share of federal revenue from the MST tended to depress the progressivity of the tax system at the top end of the income scale.

A similar effect on progressivity was generated by the substitution of the MST with a broad-based value-added tax, the Goods and Services Tax (GST). This tax shifted some of the tax burden from business imputes to consumer goods. Ruggeri and Bluck (1990) compared the two taxes and concluded that the GST is more regressive than the MST. Recognizing the reduction in progressivity, the federal government enriched substantially the sales tax credit. Whether the shift from the MST for the GST is viewed as being regressive or distributionally-neutral, therefore, depends on whether the sales tax credit is considered to be a transfer payment or an integral part of the GST structure.

The final major tax policy change involved substantial increases in payroll taxes. Since these taxes are proportional to wages but have an upper limit, increases in their rates would be distributed in a regressive pattern. Howard, Ruggeri and Van Wart (1995) show that, when added to the PIT, the combination of payroll taxes and income taxes effectively yield a proportional rate structure on labour income. It must be recognized, however, that the federal payroll taxes generate a specific entitlement to a current or future transfer benefit. Therefore, their distributional impact may be more appropriately measured by the net tax liability, after the benefits they provide have been taken into consideration.

PROVINCIAL

Similar tax changes occurred at the provincial level. By virtue of the Tax Collection Agreements, whereby the federal government collects personal income tax for all provinces except Quebec, provinces automatically parallelled the partial de-indexing of the PIT. Therefore, federal-provincial coordination in the PIT field compounded the regressive effects of the federal policy. Provincial tax progessivity was also reduced by increases in retail sales tax (RST) rates and expansion of the base. Unlike the federal changes to the MST and the shift to the GST, at the provincial level the increased regressivity was not offset by increased transfers through a sales tax credit. Finally, the increases in provincial health-care premiums and payroll taxes reduced the overall progressivity of provincial taxes.

Discretionary provincial PIT changes differed in effect from the federal changes. Provinces raised general rates, which would tend to increase the positive redistributional impact of the PIT, imposed high income surtaxes of substantial magnitudes, especially in Ontario and British Columbia, and introduced low income tax reductions. The extent to which these PIT changes offset the regressivity of other tax changes is not known. One can safely state, however, that the effect of provincial tax changes in the distribution of income since 1986 was less than that of the federal changes.

COMBINED

The general conclusion is that, with the exception of the provincial PIT adjustments, all the tax policy changes introduced since 1986 have been in the direction of decreasing the redistributional impact of the tax system. The extent to which they offset the built-in tendency of the tax system towards greater progressivity because of the dominance of the PIT and its high built-in growth is a subject for future investigation.

Purchases

FEDERAL

We estimated that, when federal purchases are assigned on the basis of income, their incidence is roughly proportional. We expect, therefore, that federal changes in government purchases did not have a significant impact on fiscal redistribution.

PROVINCIAL

Provincial spending on health care has a strong built-in growth tendency, largely because of the aging of the Canadian population. In recent years the value of services provided per capita and per patient of the same age has declined as provinces have attempted to contain this demographic pressure. To the extent that this reduction in spending resulted from genuine efficiency improvements it should have no effect on income redistribution. To the extent that it involved a reduction in the level of services provided, it redistributed total income from lower to higher income Canadians and from seniors to younger Canadians. However, since total spending on health has increased since 1986, these provincial purchases have led to greater redistribution overall.

COMBINED

With respect to combined government purchase, the direction at both federal and provincial levels has been towards reductions. Overall government purchases were found to be strongly redistributive, especially at the provincial level. To the extent that health care, in particular, has increased as a share of total purchases, these reductions are not expected to have weakened the redistributional impact of government purchases to date.

Transfers

FEDERAL

At the federal level three major initiatives altered the redistribution impact of transfers. The clawback of OAS and, later, the income-testing of the age exemption in the PIT (which can be considered a transfer payment delivered through the income tax system) reduced the level of benefits, but increased their progressivity. The repackaging of Family Allowance and the dependent credit in the PIT into an enriched Child Tax Benefit had minor redistributional effects. The redistribution impact of the reduction in UI generosity is not clear because of the interaction of efficiency and equity effects and because UI was found to be regressive in the lower income range.

PROVINCIAL

The main policy changes at the provincial level involved social assistance. The benefits per recipient have increased over the period on average and in most provinces. However, since 1993 it appears likely that average benefits have been reduced somewhat. Since spending on social assistance has increased relative to total government spending and to GDP, this has increased the degree of income redistribution. However, the recent trends suggest that this may have reversed since 1993 and social assistance policy is leading towards less redistribution.

COMBINED

On balance one may expect that the changes in transfer payments have not altered much the redistributional impact of the fiscal system, although the tendency in recent years is towards less redistribution. However, the growth of transfers as a share of government spending has had a small positive impact on fiscal redistribution.

All Fiscal Components

A detailed evaluation of the redistributional effects of all the fiscal changes since 1986 would require a complete update of this study. In our view, such an update would be more meaningful if it included the major changes introduced by all governments to eliminate or substantially reduce their deficits. A study using data for 1995, for example, would capture the major effort at deficit reduction by the federal government. At that point one would be better equipped to address the issue of how the burden of reducing the deficit was shared by the various income groups. From our cursory review one may conclude that, on the whole, fiscal policy changes since 1986 have likely generated some reduction in the degree of income redistribution delivered by the fiscal system. However, the growth in the share of PIT in total revenue and of transfers in total spending has likely more than offset this policy direction. Whether this trend will continue is yet to be seen.

NOTES

1. See, for example, Jog and Mintz (1989). Changes in effective tax rates by industry and capital asset varied widely.

Appendix

The Appendix contains a more detailed discussion of methodological issues identified in Chapter 1. The income concept, selection of government revenues and expenditures, and the measurement of incidence are discussed in detail.

THE CONCEPT OF INCOME

This study uses a comprehensive concept of income called post-government income. It is defined to include all earned income from labour and capital plus government transfer payments and the benefits of government purchases minus taxes.[1] Earned income includes both money income and imputed sources of income. It is composed of annual wages and salaries, supplementary labour income, pensions, income of unincorporated business and income from capital in the form of interest, dividends, rents and capital gains. The net income of farm operators is adjusted to include in-kind income.

The above definition of money and non-money earned income must be adjusted to remove the burden of indirect taxation that is assumed to be borne by factor earnings. The amount of taxes that are shifted backwards to labour income reduce the wages that would have been received in the absence of government fiscal activity. Therefore, the amount shifted backwards must be added to observed wages in order to obtain private income. A similar adjustment must also be made for taxes borne by owners of capital. This includes corporate income and capital taxes not shifted to consumers and labour, the employers' portion of payroll taxes, which is borne by labour, the portion of the property tax borne by capital and the indirect component of sales and excise taxes. In a small open economy this indirect component of sales and excise taxes cannot be shifted to consumers, but to the least mobile factor of production which is labour income.

This study uses a highly detailed, consistent micro database developed by Statistics Canada, the Social Policy Simulation Database/Model (SPSD/M). This database consists of a simulated sample of over 100,000 individual Canadians in their family contexts for 1986, with extensive detail on demographic composition, income sources, employment status, education and expenditures. From this database we aggregated households into 22 income classes and 15 family types, which provides a breakdown of the population into 330 distinct groups. This aggregation provides a useful population breakdown for fiscal incidence analysis and allows a reasonable cell count for each group.

The SPSD/M data was broadly adjusted to ensure that all totals agreed with and are consistent with the NIA aggregates for income components and government revenue and expenditures. The components of actual post-government income used in this study are shown in Table A-1.

SELECTION OF GOVERNMENT REVENUES AND EXPENDITURES

Our definition of the government universe is somewhat narrower than that used by Statistics Canada's National Income and Expenditure Accounts (NIA) and Financial Management System (FMS) Accounts. Government is broadly defined in these accounts to include government departments, administrative, regulatory and special funds (including working capital funds), governmental institutions (universities, hospitals, jails, etc.), agencies, Crown corporations, universal pension plans, and non-trusteed public sector pension plans. In our analysis, we have deleted Crown corporations from this broad definition of the government universe and included them in the private sector. We believe that this treatment better reflects the definition of government as a purveyor of public goods and services.

Revenues

Gross government revenues can be generated from six sources: taxation, royalties, sale of goods and services, borrowing, investment income and printing currency. However, as we explain in the following paragraphs, most revenues of relevance for fiscal incidence analysis come from taxation.

Royalties are not a tax imposed on individual incomes, assets or expenditures, but a price charged for the extraction and sale of depleted Crown resources. However, in a more general sense, royalties may be defined as a tax since these revenues

TABLE A-1: Actual Post-Government Income: Canada, 1986

Item	Adjusted NIA
A. *Private money income*	
Wages and salaries	245.368
Military pay and allowance	2.948
Net income of farm operators	3.519
Non-farm employment income (excl. rent)	17.214
Paid net rent	1.432
Cdn. dividends and miscellaneous investment	5.419
Interest received	26.864
Interest, dividends and miscellaneous investment income from non-residents	1.418
Other investment income (exc. income of trusteed pension funds and income of life insurance companies)	1.335
Pension income	
Private	6.891
Public	3.265
Other taxable income	--
Total private money income	315.700
B. *Government transfers to persons*	
Unemployment insurance benefits	10.394
CPP & QPP	7.422
OAS, GIS and provincial top-ups	13.875
Social assistance	6.280
Family allowances	2.524
Workmen's Compensation benefits	2.675
Veteran's benefits	1.158
Child Tax Credit	1.573
Sales Tax Credit	0.349
Provincial Tax Credits	1.034
Transfers from non-residents	0.777
Total direct transfers to individuals	48.061
Total family money income	363.761
C. *Non-money income additions*	
Imputed interest	3.989
Imputed rent	
Farm	0.134
Non-farm	10.049
Investment income of life insurance companies	8.197
In-kind farm income	0.198
Adjustments to farm income	0.229
Total non-money income additions	22.796

... *continued*

TABLE A-1 *(continued)*

Item	Adjusted NIA
D. Adjustments to income	
Employer's portion of payroll taxes	
UIC contributions	5.609
CPP & QPP	3.123
WCB	3.224
Payroll taxes	1.897
Health-care premiums	1.115
Supplementary labour income	11.519
Retained earnings to Canadians	8.138[a]
CIT on retained earnings	1.554
Transfers from corporations	
To charities	0.323
To bad debts	0.270
Capital gains on real estate	41.036
Indirect transfers	
Grants to charities	4.165
Special transfers	1.460[b]
Grants and scholarships	0.492
Homebuyers' grants	0.111
Miscellaneous grants	0.037
Property tax allocated on income components	6.279
Petroleum and gas revenue tax not shifted to consumers	.348
Capital tax not shifted to consumers	.383
Sales tax not shifted to consumers	4.974
Total adjustment to income	96.057
Total income before taxes and benefits of government purchases	482.614
E. Benefits of government purchases and transfers to businesses	130.166
F. Taxes borne by Canadians	166.450
Total post-government income	446.330
NIA personal income	427.262[c]

Notes:
[a]Total earnings of $13.646 minus shifted portion.
[b]Portion of NIA special transfers of $4.564 allocated to native peoples and adult training payments.
[c]Table 5, NIA, cat. 13-201.

are appropriated by the government sector from the private sector. Our analysis includes royalties as a source of government revenue.

The commercial sale of most goods and services by government is assumed to be outside the government universe and, therefore, is treated as private transactions. If these goods are sold at competitive prices, then profits can be expected to equal zero; therefore, no net revenue is generated for the provision of public goods and services. We make an exception for liquor and lottery tickets, in which the government has a legal monopoly. As discussed later, the profits from these sales are equivalent to excise taxes on the goods and will be treated as revenue from taxation.

Fees and charges levied by governments for the provision of goods and services may have the characteristics of a user price or of an excise tax. Fees and charges may be set for full or partial cost recovery for the provision of a particular service, they may be set with respect to other administrative or program criteria, or they may be set to raise net revenue, similar to liquor and lottery ticket prices. In this study we assume simply that all revenues from fees and charges are excise taxes.

Governments engage in large financial transactions, much of which is between governments (including special funds) and, therefore, generates no revenue from private sources. Financial transactions with the private sector are largely assumed to be outside of government universe, similar to the commercial sale of goods and services. Most of these operations are related to the cash flow management of revenue funds and serve no net revenue generating purpose. Only the net borrowing (lending) which is used to cover a current budget deficit (surplus) has an impact on the provision of public services and, therefore, must be considered in the analysis of the distributional impact of government fiscal activity.

A budget deficit may be treated as a current tax liability, following from the so-called Ricardian Equivalence theorem, or as a liability solely on future generations. In the latter case, the deficit can be ignored for annual tax incidence and the benefit is captured on the expenditure side. If we treat the deficit as a current tax liability, however, we must make some assumptions about the associated tax revenue.

We could assume that the deficit would be financed by raising all tax revenue by the same proportion for each tax. This approach would increase the structural progressivity of the tax system. For the tax system as a whole, the value of the global progressivity index would also increase because a proportional increase in a progressive tax raises its redistributional impact. Alternatively, we could assume that the deficit would be financed in a manner that left the relative distribution on income unchanged. This assumption would be consistent with a government policy to maintain the same relative distribution of income In this case, the estimated values of the progressivity indices, RSA_i and RSA_G, would be the same whether the deficit was included or excluded from the revenue base. Because of the arbitrary assumptions required to allocate the deficit and because the Recardian equivalence hypothesis is not generally accepted, we decided to measure the incidence of the existing taxes with respect to the revenue they raise.

Investment income from past government loans and advances to the private sector and from direct capital investments are omitted from government revenues because the fiscal benefit of this source of income is already captured on the revenue side by the concomitant reduction in the tax plus deficit burden. Likewise, it would be incorrect to net out this income from interest payments on the expenditure side because this would double-count the benefit that is already included on the revenue side.

The federal government has the additional power to raise revenue by increasing the supply of flat money. This results in a proportional increase in the price level and a redistribution of real resources from the private to public sector. We could account for this "inflation tax" by deflating post-government incomes for the change in price level over the year, assuming that inflation has no affect on the distribution of income and of taxes. As a result, the level of taxation would increase, but its structural incidence would be unaffected. However, since the Bank of Canada has pursued an explicit zero inflation rate target for monetary growth since the early 1980s and since Canadian governments have not explicitly used this power as a means to raise revenue, we will ignore it.

In conclusion, total government revenue in this study includes all taxes, royalties, profits from the sale of lottery tickets and liquor, and fees and charges. In general we will refer to this total revenue as revenue from taxation.

Total government revenue from taxation in Canada in 1986 is shown in Table A-2 for the three levels of government combined. The principal data source is Statistics Canada's (1992a) National Income and Expenditure Accounts (NIA). This is supplemented by the Financial Management System Accounts (FMS), also published by Statistics Canada (1992). The totals for each level of government and each major tax type are from the NIA, while the FMS was used to provide a more detailed desegregation of NIA tax revenues by source. The NIA framework ensures that the taxation and expenditure statistics are consistent with the total income base used for fiscal incidence.

The definition of taxes used in this study differs somewhat from the NIA for the federal and provincial levels of government. Federal tax revenues have been adjusted to include contributions to the Canada Pension Plan (CPP), while federal personal income tax revenue is grossed up to include the value of the refundable child and sales tax credits, which we define as transfer payments delivered through the income tax system. Provincial tax revenues have been adjusted to include

TABLE A-2: Total Government Revenue from Taxation, 1986

	$ Million	% of Total
Direct taxes of persons		
Personal income tax	63,102	35.98
Contributions to public pensions	3,700	2.11
Contributions to UI	9,615	5.48
Contributions to WCB	3,224	1.84
Estate taxes	13	0.01
Subtotal	79,654	45.42
Direct taxes on corporations		
Corporate income tax	14,081	8.03
Other corporate taxes	55	0.03
Subtotal	14,136	8.06
Indirect taxes		
General sales tax	24,069	13.72
Fuel taxes	4,587	2.62
Other excise taxes and duties	5,406	3.08
Customs import duties	4,169	2.38
Capital tax	1,275	0.73
Real property tax	17,438	9.94
Miscellaneous	3,359	1.92
Subtotal	60,303	34.39
Natural resource revenue		
Forestry	360	0.21
Oil and gas revenues	3,008	1.72
Mineral and potash royalties	300	0.17
Sales of Crown leases	425	0.24
Water and power rentals	335	0.19
Petroleum and gas revenue tax	437	0.25
Subtotal	4,865	2.78
Other revenue		
Provincial payroll taxes	1,897	1.08
Health insurance premiums	2,229	1.27
Liquor profits	2,149	1.23
Motor vehicle lics. and reg.	1,601	0.91
Fees and charges	1,156	0.66
Subtotal	9,032	5.15
Contributions to CPP and QPP	6,246	3.56
Lottery revenue	1,042	0.59
Hospital revenue	101	0.06
Total tax revenue	*175,379*	***100.00*

Note: **Total may not add up due to rounding

contributions to the Quebec Pension Plan (QPP) and provincial natural resources revenues have been adjusted to include royalties on Crown resources. In addition, the proceeds from lottery ticket sales and hospital revenues have been added to total provincial tax revenue. The tax revenues attributed to local governments are exactly the NIA amounts.

In the actual calculation of taxes we made two additional adjustments, for taxes paid by non-residents and for the indexing of transfer payments to individuals. Since we are estimating the incidence of Canadian taxation on Canadian residents only, we assigned to non-residents a portion of domestic revenues. However, we did not include foreign taxes paid by Canadian residents. The most important adjustment is with respect to Corporate Income Tax (CIT) revenues, where a portion of the amount assumed to be borne by capital was assigned to non-residents on the basis of the foreign share of total dividends. A similar adjustment was made for royalties.

A detailed adjustment to tax revenues assumed to be borne by consumers was made for the effect of the indexing of transfers. Following the approach discussed below, the actual indexing amounts benefiting the recipients of transfers was treated as a negative tax and, therefore, subtracted from the portion of each tax assigned to consumers and from the transfers received by households. The largest adjustment was for the consumption taxes.

Table A-2 indicates that combined federal and provincial personal income taxes accounted for 36 percent of total tax revenues in 1986, by far the single largest revenue source to government. Combined payroll taxes, including UI, CPP/QPP and WCB contributions, provincial payroll taxes, and health-care premiums (which we argue has features of both a payroll and a poll tax), accounted for 13 percent of total revenues. Thus, direct taxes on individual income comprised almost 50 percent of revenues.

Corporate income taxes, including government business enterprise, PGRT and mining and logging taxes, accounted for 8 percent of total tax revenues in 1986. In addition, capital taxes paid by corporations comprised about 1 percent of revenues.

Federal and provincial general sales taxes accounted for 14 percent of total tax revenues in 1986, the largest indirect tax source. Total excise taxes, including general sales taxes, fuel, other excise taxes, customs duties, liquor profits, motor vehicle registration, miscellaneous fees and charges, and lottery revenues, comprised 25 percent of overall tax revenues.

Real property taxes on private and commercial property, the major source of municipal revenues, comprised 10 percent of total 1986 tax revenues.

The final major tax revenue source is natural resource royalties, taxes and leases, which are largely collected by provincial governments. In 1986, total revenues from natural resources accounted for just under 3 percent of total government tax revenues. Almost 70 percent of natural resource revenues were from oil and gas.

As indicated on Table A-2, the NIA definition of direct taxes includes employee and employer contributions to public pensions. It could be argued that pension plan contributions are not a tax and that public sector pensions should not be treated differently than private pensions. However, we follow the NIA approach of including these contributions in government revenue and, therefore, including public pension payments in government expenditures. The main argument favouring this position is that pensions are incidental to wage expenditures in the provision of public services. Hence, the incidence of pension contributions and payments are a component of the fiscal impact of government. Table A-2 shows that contributions to public pensions comprised 2 percent of 1986 total tax revenues.

Expenditures

Governments spend revenue to purchase goods and services and to provide transfers, in kind and in cash, to persons and businesses. Government purchases of goods and services may be consumed in the current year or added to the stock of public capital to increase the provision of public services in future years. For annual incidence analysis we include the capital expenditures incurred within a year in the total expenditures on goods and services for that year.

Table A-3 shows a general consolidation of spending by all levels of government in Canada for 1986. The 18 expenditure categories by function are adapted from the FMS public accounts, while the actual values are based as closely as possible on known NIA aggregates and sub-aggregates. The FMS values were used in several cases to distribute NIA aggregates by these functional expenditure categories.

GOVERNMENT PURCHASES

While the NIA is the basic data source used, several modifications have been made to the NIA definitions of government purchases of goods and services. For all three levels of government, investment in fixed capital and inventories has been added to current expenditure to obtain total purchases of goods and services. Expenditures on goods and services by the CPP and QPP have been added to federal and provincial purchases of goods and services, respectively, while hospital expenditures have been added to provincial purchases. Federal and provincial grants to postsecondary educational institutions have been deducted from transfers and added to purchases.

TABLE A-3: Total Government Spending, 1986 (NIA, $ Billion)

	Goods and Services	Transfers to			Total	% of Total
		Persons	Non-Residents	Business		
General services	9.815	3.265			13.080	5.6
Protection of persons and property	18.459			0.036	18.495	7.9
Transportation and communication	9.531			3.100	12.631	5.4
Health	27.823			0.601	28.424	12.2
Social services	5.944	38.302	0.514		44.760	19.2
CPP/QPP	0.149	7.422	0.040		7.611	3.3
Education	29.368				29.860	12.8
Resource conservation and industrial development	7.689			6.337	14.026	6.0
Environment	1.436			0.470	1.906	0.8
Recreation and culture	2.660			0.430	3.090	1.3
Housing	0.768	0.111		1.515	2.394	1.0
Labour, employment and immigration	0.684	0.063		0.776	1.523	0.7
Regional planning and development	1.000			0.216	1.216	0.5
Research establishments	0.369			0.638	1.007	0.4
International assistance	1.399		1.241		2.640	1.1
Debt charges		32.199	10.555		42.754	18.4
Tax credits and rebates		2.956			2.956	1.3
Other	0.350	4.202			4.552	2.0
Total	117.443	89.012	12.350	14.119	232.924	100.0
% of Total	50.4	38.2	5.3	6.1	100.0	

It can be seen from Table A-3 that government purchases account for 50 percent of total government expenditures, $117.3 billion out of $233.4 billion in total. Three categories of government services account for almost 65 percent of total purchases. The largest single component of purchases is for education, almost $30 billion, which is 25 percent of the total. Purchases for health services absorbed almost as much, about 24 percent of the total. Protection of persons and property, which includes military, police and fire services, accounts for $18.5 billion, or almost 16 percent of total purchases. The largest component of general services purchases, almost $10 billion, is public servant pensions.

GOVERNMENT TRANSFER PAYMENTS

Transfer payments to persons and businesses account for the other 50 percent of total government spending. Since we are concerned with domestic fiscal incidence, transfer payments to non-residents, which are identified in the NIA only for federal government expenditures, have been deducted from federal transfers. Transfer payments also include CPP and QPP payments, respectively allocated to the federal and provincial governments. Interest payments on government debt paid to other levels of government are omitted from our analysis because, as pointed out above, we assume that the benefits to individuals from interest received by government is accounted for on the revenue side through a lighter tax burden.

Interest payments on outstanding government debt paid to corporations and persons is shown as a transfer to persons, following the NIA, in Table A-3.[2] However, we chose to omit these interest payments from the government expenditures allocated to households for two reasons. First, we omitted government borrowing from our estimates of the incidence of taxation (see Ruggeri et al. 1994a). Second, we are concerned with the redistributional impact of public programs within an annual incidence framework; intertemporal financing decisions may be re garded as a separate issue. Interest payments could, alternatively, be treated as an expenditure for the provision of current goods and services, like government employee salaries. However, since they are not a direct cost in the provision of a particular good or service, interest payments cannot be assigned to specific beneficiaries.

From Table A-3 it can be seen that federal transfers to non-residents accounted for less than 2 percent of total transfers in 1986. Transfers to resident persons, which includes public servant pension and debt payments, was $100 billion, or 86 percent of total transfers. Debt charges alone were almost $43 billion, 43 percent of transfers to persons. Public pension transfers to persons are shown under the general services column. They accounted for about 3 percent of transfers to persons. Of the explicit transfer programs to persons, social services was by far the largest, costing over $39 billion and accounting for just over 39 percent of total transfers to persons. The CPP/QPP programs transferred almost $7.5 billion to seniors. Total transfers to businesses, $14 billion, was 12 percent of total 1986 government transfer payments.

Allocation between Orders of Government

The incidence results are shown for the federal, provincial and local governments. The federal government sets national parameters for most transfers and expenditures. Therefore, the incidence of revenues and expenditures allocated to the federal government has a direct interpretation. However, provinces and municipalities each have their own transfer and expenditure programs. Since we have aggregated all provinces and all municipalities, our results do not apply to any particular province or municipality. They indicate the incidence of the provincial and local sectors nationally. They answer the question: How does the incidence of the average provincial (local) government expenditure structure in Canada differ from that of the federal government?

To maintain comparability with earlier studies and with the NIA we treated all intergovernmental transfers as revenue and expenditure of the recipient government. The allocation of total expenditures by order of government in 1986 is shown in appendix Table A-4. This approach assumes that the donor government acts only as a tax collector for the recipient government and exercises no control over how the funds are spent.[3]

TABLE A-4: Expenditures by Order of Government ($ Billion)

	Federal	Provincial	Local	Total
Purchases of goods and services	25.911	56.811**	34.626	117.348
Transfers to persons*	64.647	30.824	4.192	99.663
Transfers to business	7.322	6.140	.657	14.119
Total expenditure	97.880	93.775	39.475	231.130

Notes:
*Includes debt charges and CPP/QPP expenditures but excludes transfers to foreigners.
**Includes expenditures by hospitals; treats transfers to universities as purchases of goods and services.

EXCESS BURDENS AND TAX EVASION

Although we are using actual revenues, it is well-known that taxes create burdens in excess of revenues collected. We do not include the distributional impact of excess burdens in our analysis for two reasons: first, as noted by Musgrave *et al.* (1974), we do not know how these burdens are distributed; second, we want to maintain consistency with our treatment of expenditures in fiscal incidence. Since tax incidence is measured within the framework of fiscal incidence, there may also be excess benefits on the expenditure side. These excess benefits have not been included because of the arbitrariness in the calculation of their values and their distribution.

It is also well-known that the amount of tax collected is less than the total legal liability because of tax evasion. We do not include the effect of tax evasion on the distribution of the tax burden because of the lack of reliable data. This approach incorporates the assumption that evaded taxes are distributed in a distributionally-neutral manner.

THE MEASURE OF INCIDENCE

In this study we measure fiscal incidence using a structural index, the ratio of expenditures to income, and a global redistributional index.[4] The redistributional index is based on a tax incidence measure introduced by Baum (1987) under the name Relative Share Adjustment (RSA). The RSA_i measures, for the ith income class, the relative gain or loss of income as a result of the government's fiscal activity. Ruggeri, Van Wart and Cassady (1992) have shown that the RSA_i for the tax system is related to a common measure of tax incidence, the effective tax rate, in the following manner:

$$RSA_i^T = \frac{1-t_i}{1-t} \qquad (1)$$

where t is the ratio of tax payable (T) to income (Y) and i represents the ith taxpayer or income class.

The RSA_i, as defined above, measures the local redistributional impact of a given tax. It is the ratio of the actual share of the tax liability to a share which is proportional to income. As such, it offers a direct indication of the impact of a tax on the economic position of a household (or income class) would gain approximately 3 percent (0.03/1.03) of current post-government income if the given tax were replaced by one that is proportional to income.[5]

Equation (1) can be extended to fiscal incidence by replacing t_i and t with the ratio of the net fiscal benefit or loss to income (f_i and f) where, for the total population and for each income class, $f = g + tr = t$; g and tr equal the ratio of government purchases (G) and transfer payments (Tr), respectively, to income. In the case of a balanced budget, $f = 0$ and the local fiscal redistributional measure (RSA_i) is reduced to:

$$RSA_i^F = 1 + g_i + tr_i - t_i \qquad (2)$$

A value of RSA_i greater (less) than 1 indicates that the ith income class experience a relative income gain (loss) as a result of the government's fiscal activity.

For government purchases the index for each income class is:

$$RSA_i^G = \frac{1+g_i}{1+g} \qquad (3)$$

and for transfer payments the index is:

$$RSA_i^{TX} = \frac{1+tr_i}{1+tr} \qquad (4)$$

Fiscal incidence and the resulting redistribution of income can also be viewed from a global perspective. This perspective indicates whether the overall impact of taxes and expenditures is progressive (redistribution in favour of low income households), regressive (redistribution in favour of high income households) or neutral.

Ruggeri et $al.$ (1992) have shown that the RSA_i can be transformed into a global index of redistribution, RSA_G, through suitable aggregation.[6] The global index for government purchases can be calculated as

$$RSA_G = \sum_{i=1}^{n} w_i \frac{1+g_i+tr_i-t_i}{1+g+tr-t} \qquad (5)$$

where w_i are distributional weights based on income shares. These weights are calculated as

$$w_i = y_i \left(y_i + 2\sum_{j=i+1}^{n} y_j\right) \qquad (6)$$

where y_i is the share of post-government income of the ith household ($y_i = Y_i/Y$) and households are ordered by increasing income from 1 to n. A value of $RSA_G = 1$ indicates that the fisc does not alter the relative shares of income in favour of high or low income households; we call such a fisc proportional. A value of RSA_G greater (less) than 1 indicates that the fisc redistributes income from higher (lower) to lower (higher) income classes; we call such a fisc progressive (regressive). RSA_G ranges in value from 0 to 2.

TAX INCIDENCE ASSUMPTIONS

Small Open Economy Assumption

In this study, tax incidence is measured by using shifting assumptions derived explicitly with the framework of a small open economy. The small open economy assumption affects the pattern of incidence of various taxes through two basic channels: it prevents deviations between the domestic and the world rate of return on capital and it constrains the producer price of tradeable goods and services.

One of the special characteristics of a small open economy is the perfect mobility of capital, which, in the absence of transaction costs, will generate a perfectly elastic supply of capital to the domestic economy. The net rate of return on capital is determined in the world market, is independent of the level of domestic savings and must be treated as a given. However, the world rate of return faced by the domestic economy is net of the burden of the average world tax rate on capital. Therefore, in tax incidence analysis, a distinction must be made between domestic tax rates that are equal to the average world rate and differences from that rate.

With respect to the average world tax rate on capital, the entire world economy can be treated as a closed economy and capital will bear a tax burden whose magnitude depends on the elasticity of the world supply of capital. In the simplest case of a small open economy, capital mobility does not allow any domestic tax to be borne by capital, since the domestic rate of return cannot be lower than that in the world capital market. However, this conclusion is altered when a foreign tax credit is provided.

A foreign tax credit reduces the domestic tax on capital by the amount of foreign capital taxes incurred on investment income from abroad. Therefore, assuming that the foreign capital tax is fully offset by the amount of domestic capital tax collected, if domestic capital tax rates equal the average world rate, a small open economy can be treated as a closed economy for purposes of tax incidence. In this case, domestic capital will bear a portion of the domestic burden equal to the burden borne by foreign capital in the closed world economy. Any differential between the domestic and average world rates, however, has a different pattern of incidence under the closed and the small open economy assumption. In the former case, the entire tax revenue is allocated in the same manner and capital bears the burden in relation to its supply elasticity. In the latter case, capital mobility does not allow the differential domestic tax rate to be borne by capital; this component of the domestic tax is shifted.

The small open economy assumption also affects the allocation of the portion of sales and excise taxes that affect producer prices. Under the small open economy assumption, the producer prices of tradable goods and services are determined in the world market; as a result, domestic producers are price-takers. A distinction needs to be made between the direct component of sales taxes, which is levied on final consumer purchases, and the indirect component collected on business inputs, which enters the final retail price to the extent that this can be shifted forward to consumers. Direct taxes on consumers have the same incidence patterns in a closed or small open economy because they do not affect producer prices and are applied at the same rate on domestic and imported goods and services. The incidence of the indirect component collected on business inputs differs between a small open economy and a closed economy.

Since domestic producers in a small open economy are price-takers in international markets, any indirect tax on exports cannot be shifted forward to foreign consumers. Similarly, in the case of tradeable goods, domestic goods are subject to the domestic indirect tax on inputs, but imported goods are not. Competition from imported goods does not allow the indirect tax on domestic production to be passed on to domestic consumers and, therefore, it must be absorbed by domestic factors of production. This portion will be borne primarily by labour and land because capital is perfectly mobile. Domestic producers of non-tradeable goods and services, on the other hand, do not face a world producer price and, therefore, do not have to absorb the indirect component of the tax.

In conclusion, the small open economy affects the incidence of those taxes that would impose a differential burden on capital from average world rates or would affect producer prices. The burden of those tax components under perfect capital mobility and price-taking behaviours cannot be borne by either consumers or owners of capital and must be shifted to the immobile factors, labour and land. These conclusions have been used, where applicable, in our selection of shifting assumptions shown in Table A-5.

TABLE A-5: Selected Tax Incidence Assumptions

Tax	Incidence	Allocation Series
Direct taxes on persons		
Personal income tax	Those liable for tax	PIT paid per model
Contributions to public pensions	Labour	Wages and salaries per SPSD/M
Contributions to UI	Labour	UI contributions per SPSD/M
Contributions to WCB	Labour	WCB contributions per SPSD/M
Estate taxes	Property owners	House values per SPSD/M
Direct taxes on corporations		
Corporate income tax	Base case: 50% to consumers, remainder less portion exported and less dividend tax credit to owners cf capital	Portion to consumers: total consumption (SPSD/M) Portion to capital: realized capital gains per SPSD/M
	Progressive variant: 100% less portion exported and less dividend tax credit to capital	
	Regressive variant: 100% less dividend tax credit to consumers	
PGRT	50% to labour, 50% less portion exported to capital	Portion to labour: wages and salaries per SPSD/M Portion to capital: adjusted dividends per SPSD/M, money interest per SPSD/M, accrued capital gains per SPSD/M (broad capital income)
Mining and logging income taxes	Same as corporate income tax	Same as corporate income tax
Indirect taxes		
General sales tax	Tax on final purchases: 100% less portion exported less compensation on indexed transfers to consumers	Total consumption (SPSD/M)
	Tax on business purchases: tradeables to labour and capital, non-tradeables to consumers	Adjusted factor income total consumption (SPSD/M)
	Tax paid by government institutions: families	Total money income

... continued

TABLE A-5 (continued)

Tax	Incidence	Allocation Series
Indirect taxes (continued)		
Excise taxes:		
Fuel taxes	Tax on final purchases: 100% less indexed compensation on transfers to consumers	Fuel consumption (SPSD/M)
	Tax on business purchases: tradeables to labour and capital, non-tradeables to consumers	Adjusted factor income total consumption (SPSD/M)
Other excise taxes and duties	Ibid.	Total consumption (SPSD/M) and adjusted factor income
Customs import duties	Ibid.	Consumption of transportation services (SPSD/M) and adjusted factor income
Air transportation tax	Ibid.	
Tobacco taxes and duties	100% less indexed compensation on transfers to consumers of taxed goods	Tobacco consumption (SPSD/M)
Liquor taxes and duties	Ibid.	Liquor consumption (SPSD/M)
Amusement tax	Ibid.	Recreational services consumption (SPSD/M)
Race track tax		Recreational services consumption (SPSD/M)
Capital tax	Same as corporate income tax	Portion to consumers: total consumption (SPSD/M)
		Portion to capital: broad capital income (see PGRT)
Insurance premium tax		
• on life-insurance premiums	Consumers of product	Distribution from Alberta Superintendent of Insurance below $50,000; equal per family above $50,000
• on general insurance	Consumers of product	Auto insurance: value of new and used autos (SPSD/M)
		Home insurance: market value of house (SPSD/M)
		Remaining portion: equal per family
Real property tax	Base case: owner-occupied property: homeowners; residential rental property: land portion to owners, structures portion: 50% to renters. 50% to capital; commercial-industrial property: land portion to owners, structures portion: 50% to consumers, 50% to capital	To homeowners: market value of house (SPSD/M)
		To rental property owners: rental income (SPSD/M)
		Portion to renters: rental payments (SPSD/M)
		Portion to capital: broad capital income (see PGRT)
		Portion to consumers: total consumption (SPSD/M)

Miscellaneous	Progressive variant: rental and commercial structures portion 100% to capital Regressive variant: rental structures 100% to renters, commercial structures100% to consumers Consumers	Total consumption (SPSD/M)
Natural resource revenue		
Oil	100% less indexed compensation on transfers to consumers	Consumption of gasoline, grease and oil (SPSD/M)
Gas	Ibid.	Consumption of natural gas (SPSD/M)
Other oil and gas revenues	Ibid.	As oil and gas above
Forestry	Ibid.	Market value of house (SPSD/M)
Mineral royalties	Ibid.	Total consumption (SPSD/M)
Potash royalties	Ibid.	Ibid.
Sale of Crown leases	Ibid.	Ibid.
Water and power rentals	Ibid.	Ibid.
Other revenue sources		
Provincial payroll taxes	Labour	Wages and salaries (SPSD/M)
Health insurance premiums	Labour and self-employed	Portion to labour: wages and salaries (SPSD/M) Portion to self-employed: net self-employment income, non-farm plus farm (SPSD/M)
Liquor profits	Consumers of product	Liquor consumption (SPSD/M)
Motor vehicle lics. and regs.: business	Consumers of transported goods	Total consumption less consumption of services
Motor vehicle lics. and regs.: personal	Private vehicle owners	Vehicle ownership (SPSD/M)
Other fees and charges	Consumers	Total consumption (SPSD/M)
Miscellaneous	Consumers	Total consumption (SPSD/M)
Contributions to CPP and QPP	Labour	CPP/QPP contributions per SPSD/M
Lottery revenue	Consumers of product	Distribution of Vaillancourt & Grignon (1988)
Hospital revenue	Consumers of product	Purchases from hospitals (SPSD/M)

Indexing of Transfers to Persons

As mentioned in the text, the treatment of the indexing of government transfers to persons for tax-induced increases in the price level is one of two major methodological differences between our study and previous tax and fiscal incidence studies. The importance of transfers in the measurement of commodity tax incidence was brought to the fore by Browning (1978, 1985 and with Johnson 1979). Browning (1978) initially argued that transfer payments do not bear the burden of sales and excise taxes because they are indexed. Therefore, the burden of sales and excise taxes falls entirely on factor income. In response to criticism that not all transfers are indexed (McLure 1979, and Smeeding 1979), Browning (1985) re-stated his argument within the framework of a differential tax incidence model where real government expenditures, transfers as well as purchases of goods and services, are kept constant. Since transfers account for a decreasing share of total income as income increases, Browning derives a progressive pattern of incidence for sales and excise taxes by assuming that the savings ratio is constant and that transfers are fully indexed.

A reconciliation between the traditional approach and Browning's alternative has been recently proposed by Ruggeri (1993). Ruggeri shows that within the framework of differential tax incidence, where the standard of comparison is a proportional income tax applied to a comprehensive income base, transfers affect the pattern of incidence only to the extent they are indexed. Moreover, the effect of indexing is properly captured by treating the actual degree of indexing as a negative tax. Therefore, when measuring sales tax incidence, the amount of tax to be allocated is not the gross revenue but the revenue net of the portion of transfers due to indexation; this net revenue, however, is a burden on consumers and not on factor earnings.

Ruggeri's analysis shows that the traditional approach and Browning's alternative can be treated as polar cases of a general formula. Whatever the actual degree of indexing may be, the former treats transfers as if they are not indexed at all, while the latter assumes that they are fully indexed, even when they are not.

To adjust for indexing, we reviewed each of the major government transfers to persons and determined the degree to which they are indexed for price level increases. We then evaluated the effect of a rise in the normal price level on each tax by dividing the amount of revenue assigned to consumers under the various shifting assumptions by total consumer expenditures. This price level adjustment was multiplied by the degree of indexing to determine the increase in transfers caused by a tax-induced increase in the consumer price index. This indexing amount was treated as a negative tax and, therefore, was subtracted both from the tax assigned to consumers and from the transfers received by households.

TABLE A-6: Allocation of Government Transfers to Persons

	Beneficiary	Allocation
General services		
Pensions to government employees	Pension recipients	By pension income (SPSD/M)
Social services		
UI benefits	UI recipients	UI benefits received (SPSD/M)
OAS, GIS and provincial top-ups	OAS, GIS and top-up recipients	Benefits received (SPSD/M)
Social assistance	Social assistance recipients	SA received (SPSD/M)
Family allowance	Family allowance recipients	FA received (SPSD/M)
Workmen's compensation	Workmen's compensation recipients	Combined WCB and Veterans' benefits (SPSD/M) minus veterans' benefits allocated below
Veterans' benefits	Veterans	Pension income (SPSD/M) adj. for WCB
Grants to native peoples	Natives on reserve	
CPP/QPP	CPP/QPP recipients	CPP/QPP received (SPSD/M)
Housing		
Homebuyers' assistance	Low and middle income homeowners	Homeowners by value below 2nd quintile in income dist.
Labour, employment and immigration		
Adult training payments	Recipients	Adults under 65 years
Debt charges	Holders of government debt	Interest income (SPSD/M)
Tax credits and rebates		
Sales tax credit	Credit recipients	Sales tax credit received (SPSD/M)
Child tax credit	Credit recipients	Child tax credit received (SPSD/M)
Provincial tax credits	Credit recipients	
Other		
Grants to charitable organizations	Population	Per capita
Scholarships and grants	Families of postsecondary students	Families by number of postsecondary students
Miscellaneous	Population	Per capita

Corporate Income Taxes

The traditional theoretical argument regarding the incidence of the corporate income tax (CIT) assumed that all firms are profit maximizers and the supply of capital is fixed. These two assumptions ensure that the CIT is not shifted. Since, under profit maximization, firms expand production to the point where marginal revenue equals marginal cost, a tax on pure profits will not alter the profit maximizing output and price. The CIT simply reduces the level of profit and, therefore, is borne by the owners of corporate capital. If the supply of capital is fixed, the conclusion applies to both the sort and the long run. (See Harberger 1962, and Musgrave, Musgrave and Bird 1987, pp. 263-265).

If we further assume that the personal and corporate income taxes are not integrated, the burden of the CIT falls on the owners of capital in general, not simply on corporate shareholders. In the absence of integration, dividends are taxed twice while returns to capital in the unincorporated sector are taxed only once, under the personal income tax. In this case, the CIT initially reduces rates of return in the corporate sector. In the absence of transaction costs, this change will stimulate the movement of capital from the corporate sector (raising returns) to the unincorporated sector (lowering returns) until the after-CIT rates of return in the two sectors are equalized. The burden of the CIT is therefore borne by capital in general.

This conclusion does not hold to the extent that the PIT and CIT are integrated, as they are in Canada. In the Canadian tax system, partial integration is achieved through the dividend gross-up and the dividend tax credit in the PIT. The former increases the value of cash dividends to the amount that would be distributed in the absence of the CIT; the latter returns to the recipient of dividends the amount of the CIT assigned to dividends. With perfect integration, dividends do not bear the burden of the CIT; only that portion of the CIT which is not exported and which exceeds the value of the dividend tax credit imposes a burden on domestic owners of capital. This burden falls directly on retained earnings and indirectly on capital gains.

The return of equity is composed of dividends and capital gains (losses). The profits which are not distributed in a given year increase a company's net worth and create capital gains in the future. Since, under perfect integration, dividends do not bear the burden of the CIT, the domestic CIT net of the dividend tax credit represents double taxation of capital gains: they are indirectly taxed in the form of CIT on retained earnings, and then they are subject to the PIT in their realized value. Some double taxation occurs also in the unincorporated sector. The income of unincorporated business is taxed entirely under the PIT. The return on the savings of these businesses (equivalent to corporate retained earnings) is then taxed again under the PIT. Therefore, if CIT and PIT rates are very similar, the

CIT does not impose a significant differential tax burden on corporate capital and there is no inducement for capital movement from the corporate to the unincorporated sector. In conclusion, under profit maximization, with a fixed supply of capital and perfect integration between the PIT and CIT, the domestic burden of the CIT would be borne by owners of corporate capital in proportion to their capital gains.

The general theoretical conclusion that the corporate income tax (net of the dividend tax credit) is borne by the owners of capital (general or corporate only) has been challenged on various grounds.

First, it is argued that the corporate tax base is not identical to the pure profit of economic theory. Therefore, even under profit maximization the CIT will affect output decisions and may be shifted to labour or to consumers.

Second, in oligopolistic markets firms may use cost plus pricing instead of marginal cost price. In this case the CIT may be treated as any other cost of production. It will affect output and pricing decisions and may be shifted backward to labour or forward to consumers. (See Shoup 1948, and Musgrave *et al.* 1987, pp. 385-389).

Third, the pricing decisions of firms may aim at maximizing sales subject to a profit constraint. As shown by Baumol (1973, p. 326), in this situation the CIT will depress the firm's profits below the constraint level. If the firm reduces output and raises prices in order to increase the pre-tax rate of profit, the CIT shifted to consumers and to labour depending on the elasticity of the labour supply.

Fourth, even if the CIT is borne by owners of capital in the short run, in the long unit is likely to be shifted. As shown by Feldstein (1974), if savings are not fixed, but are responsive to the rate of return on capital, the CIT will be shifted backward to labour.

Under the above conditions there could be considerable shifting of the CIT. The exact shifting pattern would have to be determined empirically. Unfortunately, the empirical studies do not provide any more definite guide than the theoretical results on the incidence of the CIT. A survey of the extensive empirical literature from the 1960s is provided by Mieszkowski (1969). More recent studies are Spencer (1969), Dusanski and Tanner (1974) and Sebold (1979).

The small open economy assumption, combined with a foreign tax credit, would affect the conclusion derived for a closed economy only with respect to the difference between the domestic CIT rate and the average world corporate tax rate, as discussed above. A study for the Conference Board of Canada by Zollo and Warda (1987) on corporate tax rates in Canada, the US, Japan and the European Economic Community indicates that the Canadian rates are quite similar to those in the major industrial countries. Therefore, we can use the same shifting assumptions that would apply in the case of a closed economy.

In our calculations we selected, as a base case, a set of shifting assumptions that represent a compromise between the cases of no shifting and full forward shifting. First we allocated 50 percent of the CIT revenue (net of the petroleum and gas revenue tax) to domestic consumers; from the other half we subtracted, first, the share borne by foreign recipients of Canadian dividends and, second, the dividend tax credit; the balance was allocated to capital gains.

We also estimated the CIT incidence with no shifting and full forward shifting. In the first case, we started with the gross amount assigned to the domestic sector on the basis of its share of dividends and, then, subtracted the dividend tax credit, in order to derive the net amount allocated to capital gains. In the second case, we assigned the entire CIT revenue to consumers on the basis of total consumption, but treated the dividend tax credit as a negative tax on domestic recipients of dividend income.

In Canada, capital gains receive preferential tax treatment. Currently they are taxed only on 75 percent of their value.[7] In 1986, the inclusion rate was 50 percent. It may be argued that the partial inclusion rate serves the same purpose as the dividend tax credit, namely avoidance of double taxation of capital gains. On this basis, consistency of treatment for tax incidence purposes would require that the PIT revenue be raised by the amount lost through partial inclusion, and that this amount would then be subtracted from the CIT assigned to capital gains. Since the partial inclusion of capital gains has not been justified as a policy measure on the double taxation argument, we have not made the above adjustment, although we think that it has methodological merit.

Sales and Excise Taxes

The incidence of sales taxes is a subject of long-standing controversy among public finance economists. Some authors, notably Brown (1939) and Rolph (1952), have argued that a sales tax creates a wedge between firms' factor incomes. Therefore, a sales tax has a sources side effect only and is borne in proportion to the distribution of factor earnings. This conclusion has been rejected on a variety of grounds.

First, it can be applied only within the framework of absolute tax incidence, where a sales tax is imposed and the funds are not spent. Therefore, it measures the effect of a change in the budget position rather than the incidence of a sales tax. Second, it applies only to an all consumption model, where there is no savings and no capital formation. As shown by Musgrave et al. (1987), when this assumption is relaxed, a general sales tax on consumer goods alone increases the relative prices of consumer goods with respect to those of capital goods. As a result, consumers are made worse off relative to savers. Using the approach of differential incidence there are no effects on the sources side because replacing a proportional income tax with a general sales tax leaves factor income unchanged. Therefore, a sales tax on consumer goods only is borne entirely by consumers in accordance with the distribution of consumer expenditure.

As noted above, the case for backward shifting of sales and excise taxes has recently been reformulated by Browning (1978, 1985 and with Johnson 1979), based on the tax treatment of transfer payments. As pointed out earlier, sales and excise tax revenues must be adjusted for transfer indexing. In our calculations we performed a fairly detailed allocation of sales and excise taxes.

First, we acknowledged that a portion of the revenue from sales and excise taxes originated from business purchases (Siddiqi and Murty 1989). Under a small open economy assumption, this indirect tax component cannot be shifted forward but must be absorbed by factors of production (details for general sales taxes are found in Ruggeri and Bluck 1990 and 1992).

The direct tax component was allocated to consumers. In the case of the federal and provincial general sales taxes, this direct revenue was first allocated to each of 39 categories of consumer spending in accordance with their effective tax rates (estimated by Kuo, McGirr and Poddar 1988, adjusted to 1986). The amounts assigned to each expenditure component were then allocated to various households on the basis of their consumption of each item according to the SPSD/M micro database. This procedure yielded a detailed estimate of the tax payable before the adjustment for indexing.

Excise taxes produce an additional effect. Since they are levied on selected items they alter the relative prices of consumer goods. Therefore, their burden, net of the indexing effect, is borne by the consumers of the taxed items rather than consumers in general.

Real Property Taxes

Economists disagree on the incidence of the property tax as much as they do on the incidence of the corporate income tax. Part of the disagreement depends on whether incidence is analyzed at the national level, thus involving an average national tax rate, or at the local level. In this study we deal with the country as a whole and, therefore, measure the incidence of the average national property tax rate. The effect of property tax differentials locally or among provinces is not captured by our results.

With respect to residential property, the traditional view is that the property tax on land is borne by landowners and the tax on structures is borne by their users, namely homeowners and renters. Since land is treated as being fixed in supply, the tax is fully capitalized, as it causes a drop in the after-tax rate of return, thus imposing a burden on landowners. Structures, on the other hand, are assumed to have a perfectly elastic supply at the rate of return on capital in general.

A tax on structures would initially depress the rate of return on structures, which would then cause a flight of capital to alternative investments. The reduction in the supply of capital for investment in structures would then push the before-tax rate of return higher, until it is equalized in all sectors. Under this assumption, the property tax on structures cannot be borne by their owners, but is shifted to their users: homeowners, as recipients of housing services, and tenants.

This traditional view came under strong attack in the mid-1970s. According to the new view, initiated by Mieskowski (1972) and elaborated by Aaron (1975), land is still treated as a fixed supply and the tax on land remains a burden on landowners. With respect to structures, however, a distinction is made between the average national tax rate and local deviations from this rate.

In the new view, the average national tax is assumed to be equivalent to a tax on all capital assets. Under the assumptions that capital is perfectly mobile within the country, its supply is fixed, capital markets are perfectly competitive and the supply of structures is fixed for the country as a whole, the average national tax cannot be shifted to the users of structures, but must be borne by the owners of capital in general. The differential tax rates on structures, however, can be shifted, as they would affect relative factor and commodity prices.

The same conclusions apply to property taxes paid by firms. The overall supply of land is fixed, therefore, the burden of land taxes falls on the owners of land independently of the use of the land. The incidence of the property tax on structures will fall on consumers under the traditional view that the supply of structures is perfectly elastic, and on capital income according to the new view that the supply of structures is fixed for the nation as a whole.

The small open economy assumption does not affect the incidence of the property tax on land because its domestic supply is fixed. The only difference is that, unlike the closed economy case, part of the tax can be exported to the extent that the land is owned by foreigners. In the case of owner-occupied residential structures, the incidence assumptions are not affected because those structures are strictly complementary to internationally immobile labour. Residential rental structures are an investment good and are subject to the restriction that the after-tax world rate of return on capital is fixed, which implies forward shifting even under the new view. Since residential rental services can be considered non-tradeable, the domestic rate is fully shifted forward to renters.

Business structures are used to produce both tradeable as well as non-tradeable goods and services. Since the prices of tradeable goods and services are fixed in the world market, the domestic property tax that would be assigned to them cannot be borne either by capital or by consumers and, therefore, represents a burden on labour.

In this study, we divided the property tax revenue into three major components according to the source of the payment: residential homeowners, residential rental properties and commercial-industrial properties.

The tax collected from homeowners was allocated entirely to them in accordance with the value of the property. This approach is theoretically consistent with the new view of property taxation. However, in our case it yields the same results as the traditional view because imputed rent, which represents a measure of housing services consumption, was allocated as a proportion of the value of the residential property.

Residential rental properties and commercial-industrial properties share a common feature: they serve to produce goods and services for sale to consumers. The issue then is whether the property tax on these structures should be treated as equivalent to an excise tax (traditional view) or as corporate income tax (new view). As in the case of the corporate income tax, we used a compromise approach between the two polar views. We assumed that neither the supply of structures nor the supply of capital is perfectly inelastic and, therefore, allow for some forward shifting of the property tax on business structures. Specifically, the land component was allocated to the owners (recipients of rental income in the case of residential rental properties and recipients of capital income for the rest) and the revenue from the tax on structures was allocated in equal proportion to consumers in general (renters in the case of residential rental properties) and recipients of capital income.

TABLE A-7: Allocation of Transfers to Business

	Beneficiary	Allocation
Agriculture	Farmers	Net farm income
Health	Case 1: by money income Case 2: population	Case 1: private income plus transfers Case 2: per capita
Housing	Homeowners and renters	50% homeowners, 50% renters by value of housing
Other business	Consumers	Expenditures on total consumption

TABLE A-8: Allocation of Government Expenditures
Allocation of Expenditures on Goods and Services

	Beneficiary	Allocation
General services	Case 1: by money income	Case 1: private income plus transfers
	Case 2: population	Case 2: per capita
Protection of persons and property	Case 1: by money income	Case 1: private income plus transfers
	Case 2: population	Case 2: per capita
Transportation and communications		
Roads, streets and snow removal	2/3 users (commercial shifted to consumers)	2/3 to expenditures on passenger vehicles
	1/3 non-users	1/3 to total consumption less services
		60% by house values, 40% by rent
Parking	Passenger vehicles	Expenditure on passenger vehicles
Air, rail and water	50% passengers	Expenditures on purchased transportation
	50% consumers	Expenditures on total consumption less services
Public transit	Users	Expenditures on purchased transportation
Postal	Users	Expenditures on communications
Telecommunications	Users	Expenditures on communications
Other	Users	Expenditures on transportation and communications
Health		
Hospital care	Users	Population by age, utilization and income
Medical care	Users	Population by age, utilization and income
Public health and other	Case 1: by money income	Case 1: private income plus transfers
	Case 2: population	Case 2: per capita
Social services	Transfer recipients	In proportion to transfers under this group
CPP/QPP	Transfer recipients	In proportion to transfers under this group

Education		
Elementary and secondary	Families of elementary and secondary students	Families by number of children in age group
Postsecondary	Families of postsecondary students	Families by number of postsecondary students
Retraining	Employed adults	Adults under 65 years
Other	Case 1: by money income	Case 1: private income plus transfers
	Case 2: population	Case 2: per capita
Resource conservation and industrial development		
Agriculture	Farmers and consumers	50% to farm net income
		50% to food consumption
Other	Business and consumers	50% to interest, dividends and rent
		50% to total consumption
Environment		
Pollution control	Case 1: by money income	Case 1: private income plus transfers
	Case 2: population	Case 2: per capita
Water, sewerage and garbage	Households and business (shifted to consumers)	2/3 to households, adjusted for size
		1/3 to total consumption
Recreation and culture	Case 1: by money income	Case 1: private income plus transfers
	Case 2: population	Case 2: per capita
Housing	Low and middle income homeowners and renters	50% homeowners, 50% renters by value below
		2nd quintile in income distribution
Labour, employment and immigration	Users of services	Adults under 65 years
Regional planning and development		
Planning, zoning and community dev.	Homeowners	House values
Regional development	Case 1: by money income	Case 1: private income plus transfers
	Case 2: population	Case 2: per capita
Research establishments	Case 1: by money income	Case 1: private income plus transfers
	Case 2: population	Case 2: per capita
International assistance	Foreign citizens	None allocated
Other	Case 1: by money income	Case 1: private income plus transfers
	Case 2: population	Case 2: per capita

NOTES

1. This is equivalent to Gillespie's (1966, 1980) concept of "adjusted broad income."
2. Interest payments on government debt paid to other orders of government are omitted.
3. Alternatively, since a large proportion of intergovernmental transfers are earmarked by the donor for specific purposes, they can be allocated to the donor government. The FMS accounts allocate both revenue and expenditure for specific purpose transfers to the donor government, but treat the general purpose transfers in the same manner as the NIA.
4. See Ruggeri, Van Wart and Cassady (1992) for the derivation of redistributional indices from structural indices of tax incidence.
5. It should be noted that the rate of change of equation (1) is a constant proportion of the rate of change of g_i or tr_i. Therefore, the rate of change of the local redistributional index, RSA_i, provides the same information about the progressivity of expenditures as the slope of the structural indices, g_i or tr_i.
6. Details on the properties of RSA_G and a comparison with other progressivity measures are also found in Cassady, Ruggeri and Van Wart (1992).
7. Prior to February 2, 1995 this was in excess of a general $100,000 lifetime capital gains exemption. Small business owners and farmers receive a $500,000 lifetime capital gains exemption.

References

Aaron, H. (1975), *Who Pays the Property Tax? — A New View* (Washington, DC: The Brookings Institution).

Aaron, H. and M. McGuire (1970), "Public Goods and Income Distribution," *Econometrica* 38: 907-918.

Baily, M.N., G. Burtless and R.E. Litan (1993), *Growth with Equity* (Washington, DC: The Brookings Institution).

Battle, K. and S. Torjman (1994), "The Welfare Wall: An Analysis of the Welfare/Tax System in Ontario," in *Taxation and the Distribution of Income,* ed. A.M. Maslove (Toronto: University of Toronto Press).

Baum, S.R. (1987), "On the Measurement of Tax Progressivity: Relative Share Adjustment," *Public Finance Quarterly* 15: 166-187.

Baumol, W.J. (1973), *Economic Theory and Operations Analysis,* 3d ed. (Englewood Cliffs, NJ: Prentice-Hall).

Bjerke, K. and S. Brodersen (1978), "Studies of Income Redistribution in Denmark for 1963 and 1971," *The Review of Income and Wealth* 24 (June).

Blackburn, M. and D.E. Bloom (1985), "What is Happening to the Middle Class?" *American Demographics*.

Bordt, M., G.J. Cameron, S.F. Gribble, B.D. Murphy, G.T. Rowe and M.C. Wolfson (1990), "The Social Policy Simulation Database and Model: An Integrated Tool for Tax/ Transfer Policy Analysis," *Canadian Tax Journal/ Revue Fiscale Canadienne* 38: 48-65.

Brennan, G. (1976), "The Distributional Implications of Public Goods," *Econometrica* (March).

Browning, E.K. (1978), "The Burden of Taxation," *Journal of Political Economy* 86: 649-671.

_____ (1985), "Tax Incidence, Indirect Taxes, and Transfers," *National Tax Journal*: 38, 525-533.

Browning, E.K. and W.R. Johnson (1979), *The Distribution of the Tax Burden* (Washington, DC: American Enterprise Institute).

Buhmann, B., L. Rainwater, G. Schmaus and T.M. Smeeding (1988), "Equivalency Scales, Well-Being, Inequality, and Poverty: Sensitivity Estimates Across 10 Countries Using the Luxembourg Income Study (LIS) Database," *Review of Income and Wealth* 34: 115-142.

Business Week (Aug. 15, 1994), "Inequality: How the Gap Between Rich and Poor Hurts the Economy" (McGraw Hill) 78-83.

Calvo, G.A. (1979), "Quasi-Walrasian Theories of Unemployment," *American Economic Review* 69: 102-106.

Card, D.E. and W. C. Riddell (1993), "A Comparative Analysis of Unemployment in Canada and the United States," in *US and Canadian Labor Markets,* ed. D.E. Card and R.B. Freeman (Chicago: University of Chicage Press).

Cassady, K., G.C. Ruggeri and D. Van Wart (1992), "On the Classification and Interpretation of Progressivity Measures," (Calgary: Alberta Treasury, mimeo).

Central Statistical Office (annual) "The Effect of Taxes and Benefits on Household Income," *Economic Trends* (London: Central Statistical Office).

Corak, M. (1993), "Unemployment Insurance Once Again: The Incidence of Repeat Participation in the Canadian UI Program," *Canadian Public Policy* 19: 162-176.

_____ (1994), "Unemployment Insurance, Work Disincentives, and the Canadian Labor Market: An Overview," in *Unemployment Insurance: How to Make It Work,* ed. J. Richards and W.G. Watson (Toronto: C.D. Howe Institute).

Courchene, T.J. (1994), *Social Canada in the Millennium* (Toronto: C.D. Howe Institute).

Dahlby, B.G. (1985), "The Incidence of Government Expenditures and Taxes in Canada: A Survey," in *Income Distribution and Economic Security in Canada*, ed. F. Vaillancourt (Toronto: University of Toronto Press).

_____ (1993), "Payroll Taxes," in *Business Taxation in Canada,* ed. A.M. Maslove, Ontario Fair Tax Commission Research Studies (Toronto: University of Toronto Press).

Dahlby, B.G. and G.C. Ruggeri (1995), "The Marginal Cost of Redistribution: Comment," *Public Finance Quarterly.*

Davies, J.B., F. St-Hilaire and J. Whalley (1984), "Some Calculations of Lifetime Tax Incidence," *The American Economic Review* 74: 633-649.

Deutches Institut für Wirtschaftsforschung (1983), *Wochenbericht* 30/83, July.

Diamond, P.A. (1981), "Mobility Costs, Frictional Unemployment and Efficiency," *Journal of Political Economy* 87: 798-812.

_____ (1984), *A Search Equilibrium Approach to the Microfoundations of Economics* (Cambridge, MA: MIT Press).

Dodge, D.A. (1975), "Impact of Tax, Transfer, and Expenditure Policies of Government on the Distribution of Personal Income in Canada," *Review of Income and Wealth* 21: 1-52.

Falkingham, J., J. Hills and C. Lessof (1992), "Life's Rich Rewards," *Financial Times* (London), Dec. 2.

Farmer, R.E.A. (1993), *The Macroeconomics of Self-Fulfilling Prophesies* (Cambridge, MA: MIT Press).

Feldstein, M. (1974), "Tax Incidence with Growth and Variable Factor Supply," *Quarterly Journal of Economics* 79: 551-573.

Fitoussi, J.-P. (1994), "Wage Distribution and Unemployment: The French Experience," *American Economic Review* 84: 59-64.

Fortin, P. (1994), "A Strategy for Deficit Control Through Faster Growth," *Canadian Business Economics* 3: 3-26.

Foulon, A. and G. Hatchuel (1979), "The Redistribution of Public Funds in France in 1965 and 1970," *The Review of Income and Wealth* 25.

Franzén, T., K. Lövgren and I. Rosenberg (1975), "Redistributional Effects of Taxes and Public Expenditures in Sweden," *Swedish Journal of Economics*, March.

Fullerton, D. and D.L. Rogers (1991a), "Lifetime versus Annual Perspectives on Tax Incidence," *National Tax Journal* 54: 277-288.

_____ (1991b): *Who Bears the Lifetime Tax Burden?* (Washington, DC: The Brookings Institution).

Gale, W.G. and J.K. Scholz (1994), "Intergenerational Transfers and the Accumulation of Wealth," *Journal of Economic Perspectives* 8, 4: 145-160.

Gillespie, W. (1966), *The Incidence of Taxes and Public Expenditures in the Canadian Economy*, Study No. 2 for the Royal Commission on Taxation (Ottawa: Queen's Printer).

_____ (1978), *In Search of Robin Hood, The Effect of Federal Budgetary Policies during the 1970s on the Distribution of Income in Canada* (Ottawa: C.D. Howe Research Institute).

_____ (1980a), *The Redistribution of Income in Canada* (Toronto: Gage Publishing).

_____ (1980b), "Taxes, Expenditures and the Redistribution of Income in Canada, 1951-1977," in *Reflections on Canadian Incomes* (Ottawa: Economic Council of Canada).

The Globe and Mail (Aug. 19, 1994), "The Bronx in Frankfurt" (Toronto) A10.

Government of Alberta (1987), *Superintendent of Insurance, 1987 Annual Report (Business of 1986)* (Edmonton: Alberta Consumer and Corporate Affairs).

Government of Canada (1987), *Public Accounts of Canada, 1985-86, 1986-87* (Ottawa: Queen's Printer).

_____ (1994), *From Unemployment Insurance to Employment Insurance* (Ottawa: Supply and Services Canada).

Green, C. (1994), "What Should We Do with the UI System?" in *Unemployment Insurance: How to Make It Work,* ed. J. Richards and W.G. Watson (Toronto: C.D. Howe Institute).

Greenwald, B.C. and J. Stiglitz (1988), "Examining Alternative Macroeconomic Theories," *Brookings Papers on Economic Activity* 1: 207-270.

Gross, D.M. (1994), "Unemployment and UI schemes in Europe," in *Unemployment Insurance: How to Make It Work,* ed. J. Richards and W.G. Watson (Toronto: C.D. Howe Institute).

Harberger, A.C. (1962), "The Incidence of the Corporation Income Tax," *Journal of Political Economy*; reprinted in Harberger (1974) *Taxation and Welfare* (Boston: Little Brown).

Harding, A. (1993), "Lifetime vs Annual Tax-Transfer Incidence: How Much less Progressive?" *Economic Record* 69: 179-191.

Health and Welfare Canada (1991), *Inventory of Income Security Programs in Canada, July 1990* (Ottawa: Minister of Supply and Services Canada).

Horry, I. and M. Walker (1994), *Government Spending Facts Two* (Vancouver: The Fraser Institute).

Horry, I., F. Palda and M. Walker (1994), *Tax Facts 9* (Vancouver: The Fraser Institute).

Howard, R., G.C. Ruggeri and D. Van Wart (1995), "Federal Tax Changes and Marginal Tax Rates, 1986 and 1993," *Canadian Tax Journal* 43: 906-922.

Howitt, P. (1983), "Aggregate Supply with Costly Search and Recruiting," unpublished paper presented at McMaster University Macroeconomics Conference.

Howitt, P. and R. Preston Mcfee (1987), "Costly Search and Recruiting," *International Economic Review* 28: 89-107.

Iacobacci, M. and L. Grignon (1993), "A Primer on Job Creation Schemes," (Ottawa: Department of Finance, mimeo).

James, S. (1991), "Hysteresis and the Natural Rate of Unemployment in Canada" (Ottawa: Department of Finance, mimeo).

Jog, V.M. and J. Mintz (1989), "Corporate Tax Reform and its Economic Impact: An Evaluation of Phase 1 Proposals," in *The Economic Impacts of Tax Reform,* ed. J. Mintz and J. Whalley (Toronto: Canadian Tax Papers No. 84, Canadian Tax Foundation).

Johnson, J.A. (1968), *The Incidence of Government Revenue and Expenditures*, a study for the Ontario Committee on Taxation (Toronto: Queen's Printer).

Kotlikoff, L. (1992), *Generational Accounting* (New York: The Free Press).

Krupp, H.J. (1983), "Problems of Measuring Volume, Distributional Impact and Effects of the Transfer System: The Experience of the German Transfer Enquiry Committee," paper presented to the 18th General Conference of the International Association for Research in Income and Wealth, Luxembourg, August 1983.

Kuo, C.-Y., T.C. McGirr and S.N. Poddar (1988), "Measuring the Non-Neutralities of Sales and Excise Taxes in Canada," *Canadian Tax Journal/ Revue Fiscale Canadienne* 36: 655-670.

Lambert, P.J. (1985), "The Redistributive Effect of Taxes and Benefits," *Scottish Journal of Political Economy* 32: 34-54.

Lambert, P.J. and W. Pfähler (1986), "On Aggregate Measures of the Net Redistributive Impact of Taxation and Government Expenditure," Working Paper 87 (Institute for Fiscal Studies).

Layard, R., and S. Nickell (1987), "The Performance of the British Labour Markets," in *The Performance of the British Economy,* ed. R. Dornbusch and R. Layard (Oxford: Clarendon).

Lazar, F. (1994), "UI as a Redistributive Scheme and Automatic Fiscal Stabilizer," in *Unemployment Insurance: How to Make It Work,* ed. J. Richards and W.G. Watson (Toronto: C.D. Howe Institute).

Levy, F. and R.J. Murnane (1992), "U.S. Earnings Levels and Earnings Inequality, A Review of Recent Trends and Proposed Explanations," *Journal of Economic Literature* 30: 1333-1381.

Marzouk, M.S. (1991), "Aging, Age-Specific Health Care Cost and the Future Health Care Burden in Canada," *Canadian Public Policy* 17: 490-506.

McLure, C. (1979), "Commentary," in *Income Inequality*, ed. J.R. Moroney (Lexington, MA: D.C. Heath).

Mieszkowski, P. (1972), "The Property Tax: An Excise Tax or a Profits Tax," *Journal of Public Economics* 1: 73-96.

Milbourne, R.D., D. Purvis and D Schoones (1991), "Unemployment Insurance and Unemployment Dynamics," *Canadian Journal of Economics* 24: 804-826.

Morisette, R., J. Myles and G. Picot (1994), "Earnings Inequality and the Distribution of Working Time in Canada," *Canadian Business Economics* 2: 3-16.

Murphy, B., R. Finnie and M.C. Wolfson (1994), "A Profile of High-Income Ontarians," in *Taxation and the Distribution of Income,* ed. A.M. Maslove (Toronto: University of Toronto Press).

Musgrave, R.A. (1993), "Horizontal Equity, Once More," *National Tax Journal* 43: 113-122.

Musgrave, R.A. and T. Thin (1948), "Income Tax Progression, 1929-48," *Journal of Political Economy* 56: 498-514.

Musgrave, R.A., K.E. Case and H. Leonard (1974), "The Distribution of Fiscal Burdens and Benefits," *Public Finance Quarterly* 2: 259-311.

Musgrave, R.A., P.B. Musgrave and R.M. Bird (1987), *Public Finance in Theory and Practice* Can. ed. (Toronto: McGraw-Hill Ryerson).

Nakamura, A., J. Cragg and K. Sayers (1994), "The Case for Disentangling the Insurance and Income Assistance Roles of Unemployment Insurance," *Canadian Business Economics* 3: 46-53.

Nolan, B. (1981), "Redistribution of Household Income in Ireland by Taxes and Benefits," *The Economic and Social Review* (October).

O'Connell, P.J. (1982), "The Distribution and Redistribution of Income in the Republic of Ireland," *The Economic and Social Review* (July).

O'Higgins, M. and P. Ruggles (1981), "The Distribution of Public Expenditures and Taxes Among Households in the United Kingdom," *Review of Income and Wealth* 27: 298-326.

Okun, A. (1975), *Equality and Efficiency: The Big Tradeoff* (Washington, DC: The Brookings Institution).

Ontario Fair Tax Commission (1993), *Fair Taxation in a Changing World: Highlights* (Toronto: University of Toronto Press).

Osberg, L. (1981), *Economic Inequality in Canada* (Toronto: Butterworth & Co.).

_____ (1993), "Unemployment Insurance and Unemployment Revisited" Working Paper No. 93-04, Halifax: Dalhousie University.

_____ (1994a) "What's Fair? The Problem of Equity in Taxation," in *Fairness in Taxation: Exploring the Principles,* ed. A.M. Maslove (Toronto: University of Toronto Press).

_____ (1994b), "Concepts of Unemployment and the Structure of Unemployment" Working Paper No. 94-11, Halifax: Dalhousie University.

Payette, M. and F. Vaillancourt (1986), "L'incidence des recettes et dépenses gouvernementales au Québec en 1981," *L'Actualité Économique* 62: 409-441.

Pechman, J.A. (1985), *Who Pays the Taxes, 1966-85?* Studies of Government Finance (Washington, DC: The Brookings Institution).

Pechman, J.A. and B.A. Okner (1974), *Who Bears the Tax Burden?* (Washington, DC: The Brookings Institution).

Persson, T. and G. Tabellini (1994), "Is Inequality Harmful to Growth?" *American Economic Review* 79: 325-330.

Pfähler, W. (1987), "Redistributive Effects of Tax Progressivity: Evaluating a General Class of Aggregate Measures," *Public Finance/ Finances Publiques* 42: 1-31.

Phelps, E.S. (1968), "Money-Wage Dynamics and Labor Market Equilibrium," *Journal of Political Economy* 76: 678-711.

_____ (1994a) *Structural Slumps* (Cambridge, MA: Harvard University Press).

_____ (1994b), "Low-Wage Employment Subsidies versus the Welfare State," *American Economic Review* 84: 54-58.

Phipps, S.A. (1993), "Does Unemployment Insurance Increase Unemployment?" *Canadian Business Economics* 1: 37-50.

Pissarides, C. (1990), *Equilibrium Unemployment Theory* (London: Basil Blackwell).

Poterba, J.M. (1989), "Lifetime Incidence and the Distributional Burden of Excise Taxes," *American Economics Review* 79: 325-330.

Reynolds, M. and E. Smolensky (1977), *Public Expenditures, Taxes, and the Distribution of Income: The United States, 1950, 1961, 1970* (New York: Academic Press).

Revenue Canada (1993), *Taxation Statistics* (Ottawa: Supply and Services Canada).

Robson, W.B.P. (1994), *Digging Holes and Hitting Walls: Canada's Fiscal Prospects in the Mid-1990's* (Toronto: C.D. Howe Institute).

Ruggles, P. and M. O'Higgins (1981), "The Distribution of Public Expenditures and Taxes Among Households in the United States," *Review of Income and Wealth* 27: 137-163.

Ruggeri, G.C. (1993), "On the Measurement of Sales Tax Incidence in the Presence of Transfers," *Public Finance/ Finances Publiques* 48: 132-137.

Ruggeri, G.C. and K. Bluck (1990), "On the Incidence of the Manufacturer's Sales Tax and the Goods and Services Tax," *Canadian Public Policy/Analyse de Politiques* 16: 359-373.

_____ (1992), "The Treatment of Transfers in the Measurement of Sales Tax Incidence: The Case of Canada's Manufacturers' Sales Tax," *Public Finance Quarterly* 20: 24-46.

Ruggeri, G.C. and D. Hermanutz (1995), *Leviathan Revisited, The Growth of Government Spending in Canada since 1961* (Calgary: Alberta Treasury, mimeo).

Ruggeri, G. C., D. Van Wart and K. Cassady (1992), "Global Progressivity Indices as Aggregates of Local Indices: The Relative Share Adjustment and Suits' Index," Research Paper No. 92-24 (Edmonton: Department of Economics, University of Alberta).

Ruggeri, G.C., R. Howard and K. Bluck (1994), "The Incidence of Low Income Among the Elderly," *Canadian Public Policy/ Analyse de Politiques* 20: 138-151.

Ruggeri, G.C., D. Van Wart and R. Howard (1994*a*), "The Redistributional Impact of Taxation in Canada," *Canadian Tax Journal/ Revue Fiscale Canadienne* 42: 417-451.

_____ (1994*b*), *The Redistributional Impact of Government Spending and Taxation in Canada* (Alberta Treasury, mimeo).

Sharif, N. and S. Phipps (1994), "The Challenge of Child Poverty," *Canadian Business Economics* 2: 17-30.

Shoup, Carl S. (1948), "Incidence of the Corporation Income Tax: Capital Structure and Turnover Rates," *National Tax Journal* 11.

Siddiqi, Y. and P.S.K. Murty (1989), "Commodity Indirect Taxes in the Canadian Input-Output Accounts," Ottawa: Statistics Canada, Input-Output Division, mimeo.

Smeeding, T.M. (1979), "Are Sales Taxes Progressive?" Institute for Research on Poverty, Discussion Paper, pp. 545-579.

Smeeding, T.M., P. Saunders, J. Cody, S. Jenkins, J. Fritzell, A.J.M. Hagenaars, R. Hauser and M. Wolfson (1993), "Poverty, Inequality, and Family Living Standards Impacts Across Seven Nations: The Effect of Noncash Subsidies for Health, Education and Housing," *Review of Income and Wealth* 39: 229-256.

Smith, R.S. (1986), "Flat Rate Tax Potential: A Preliminary Comparison of Three Countries," *Canadian Tax Journal* 34: 825-840.

Snower, D.J. (1994), "Converting Unemployment Benefits into Unemployment Subsidies," *American Economic Review* 84: 65-70.

Solop, S.C. (1979), "A Model of the Natural Rate of Unemployment, "*American Economic Review* 69: 117-25.

Statistics Canada (1992*a*), *National Income and Expenditure Accounts, Annual Estimates 1979-1990*, Catalog No. 13-201 Annual (Ottawa).

_____ (1992*b*), *Historical Federal Government Expenditure, 1974/75 to 1990/91*, Financial Management System basis data (Ottawa: Supply and Services Canada).

_____ (1992*c*), *Historical Federal Government Revenue 1974/75 to 1990/91*, Financial Management System basis data (Ottawa: Supply and Services Canada).

_____ (1992*d*), *Historical Provincial/Territorial Government Revenue and Expenditure 1974/75 to 1990/91*, Financial Management System basis data (Ottawa: Supply and Services Canada).

_____ (1992*e*), *Historical Local Government Revenue and Expenditure 1974/75 to 1990/91*, Financial Management System basis data (Ottawa: Supply and Services Canada).

_____ (1993), *Income Distribution by Size*, Catalog No. 13-207 Annual (Ottawa: Supply and Services Canada).

_____ (1995), *National Income and Expenditure Accounts, Annual Estimates 1983-1994* (Ottawa: Supply and Services Canada).

Stiglitz, J.E. (1974), "Wage Determination and Unemployment in LDCs," *Quarterly Journal of Economics* 88: 194-227.

Suominen, R. (1979), "Empirical Results Concerning Vertical and Horizontal Redistribution in Finland," *Review of Income and Wealth* 25: 83-103.

Thurow, L. (1984), "The Disappearance of the Middle Class," *New York Times*, Feb. 5, p. 2.

Vaillancourt, F. and J. Grignon (1988), "Canadian Lotteries as Taxes: Revenues and Incidence," *Canadian Tax Journal/ Revue Fiscale Canadienne* 36: 369-388.

Van Wart, D.C. (1994), "Transaction Externalities and Hysteresis in Labour Markets," PhD Dissertation, Simon Fraser University, Burnaby, BC.

Van Wart, D.C. and G.C. Ruggeri (1990), "The Effects of Tax Reform on the Income Elasticity of the Personal Income Tax," *Canadian Tax Journal* 38: 1210-1226.

Vermaeten, F., W.I. Gillespie and A. Vermaeten (1994), "Tax Incidence in Canada," *Canadian Tax Journal/ Revue Fiscale Canadienne* 42: 348-416.

Wolfson, M.C. (1994), "Divergent Inequalities — Theory, Empirical Results and Prescriptions," paper presented at the conference "Contemporary Issues in Income Distribution Research," University of New South Wales, Australia, Dec. 3, 1994.

Woolley, F. (1994), "Ending Universality: the Case of Child Benefits," unpublished paper presented at the 1994 Annual Meeting of the Canadian Economics Association.

OTHER SOCIAL POLICY TITLES

from the

SCHOOL OF POLICY STUDIES

Social Policy in the Global Economy, edited by Terrance M. Hunsley
(xvi, 184pp) ISBN: 0-88911-637-7
(December 1992)

The Future of Fiscal Federalism, edited by Keith G. Banting,
Douglas M. Brown and Thomas J. Courchene
(x, 368pp) ISBN: 0-88911-657-1
(June 1994)

*A New Social Vision for Canada? Perspectives on the Federal Discussion
Paper on Social Security Reform*, edited by Keith Banting and Ken Battle
(x, 140pp) ISBN: 0-88911-687-3
(December 1994)

Redefining Social Security, by Patrick Grady, Robert Howse and
Judith Maxwell (viii, 162pp) ISBN: 0-88911-714-4
(May 1995)

Labour Market Polarization and Social Policy Reform,
edited by Keith G. Banting and Charles M. Beach
(xiv, 258pp) ISBN: 0-88911-667-9
(May 1995)

All publications of the School of Policy Studies are available from:

Renouf Publishing Co. Ltd.
1294 Algoma Road
Ottawa, Ontario K1B 3W8
Tel (613) 741-4333 / Fax (613) 741-5430